ONE DAY'S GLEANINGS FROM A SMALL BACK-YARD GARDEN—SHOWING THAT INTENSIVE CULTURE CAN DO MUCH ON EVEN A SMALL SPACE

THE
BIGGLE GARDEN BOOK

VEGETABLES, SMALL FRUITS AND
FLOWERS FOR PLEASURE
AND PROFIT

BY

JACOB BIGGLE

———

ILLUSTRATED

———

*"A good garden saves doctor bills, drives away the
blues, sweetens up the home, and puts
money in thy purse."*

———

Skyhorse Publishing

Skyhorse Publishing books may be purchased in bulk at special discounts for sales promotion, corporate gifts, fund-raising, or educational purposes. Special editions can also be created to specifications. For details, contact the Special Sales Department, Skyhorse Publishing, 307 West 36th Street, 11th Floor, New York, NY 10018 or info@skyhorsepublishing.com.

Skyhorse® and Skyhorse Publishing® are registered trademarks of Skyhorse Publishing, Inc.®, a Delaware corporation.

Visit our website at www.skyhorsepublishing.com.

10 9 8 7 6 5 4 3 2 1

Library of Congress Cataloging-in-Publication Data is available on file.

ISBN: 978-1-62636-144-7

Printed in China

PREFACE

IN reality a preface is rather a queer thing, because it's a "fore-word" which is written *last!* So, it seems, I am now to have the last word. To begin, I feel especially indebted to R. L. Watts for several extracts from his excellent Pennsylvania Bulletin No. 147; to W. N. Hutt, author of Maryland Bulletin No. 116; and to the authors of various other bulletins, books and catalogs whose writings have given me occasional lifts over rough places. My thanks go also to the E. A. Strout Co., New York City, and to a few well-known implement manufacturers, who kindly loaned me several photographs. Most of the pictures in the book, however, were especially made for it by expert photographers and engravers who were carefully instructed regarding the practical details of each picture.

Now just a few hints about the final problem of the average gardener—the selling end of the business: Don't ship to every strange commission house that solicits your consignment. Get a good solid house and stick to it. Or sell direct to storekeepers; or join or form a co-operative shipping and selling association; or work up a list of retail customers of your own. As an aid to the latter plan, the Long Island Agronomist, Huntington, N. Y., has evolved a shipping package which it calls a "home hamper." It measures twenty-four inches long, fourteen inches wide, ten inches deep, and weighs about thirty pounds when filled. It contains six baskets holding about one-half peck each; these are filled with vegetables in season, from radishes to cauliflower. Assortment is made to furnish soup, salad and substantials, with occasional fancies, such as eggplant and cantaloupes. Home hampers are packed in the morning, shipped by express at 7 A. M., and delivered at the customer's door in time for dinner; hence real sweet corn, crisp lettuce, melting peas, beans, etc., all A No. 1, are available for the table of the city dweller. The average family uses two home hampers per week. Price, $1.50 each, delivered at the door, within the delivery limits of the Long Island Express Company and payable at the end of each month. Good idea, it seems to me. Try it.

Send only fresh, clean, attractive products to market; sort, grade and honestly pack and mark each package; give full measure; use only clean, neat packages, and put your name and brand thereon. Keep the "culls" for stock feed; earn a reputation for fancy products only.

My earnest wish: May your garden be a great success, whether planned for pleasure or profit.

Elmwood.   JACOB BIGGLE.

CONTENTS

NEVER PLOW SOIL WHEN IT IS VERY WET AND STICKY—WAIT UNTIL IT DRIES INTO CRUMBLY, WORKABLE CONDITION

CHAPTER I

PREPARATION OF THE LAND

It is well to aim high even when getting ready to plant things in the ground.—Harriet.

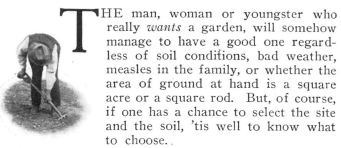

THE man, woman or youngster who really *wants* a garden, will somehow manage to have a good one regardless of soil conditions, bad weather, measles in the family, or whether the area of ground at hand is a square acre or a square rod. But, of course, if one has a chance to select the site and the soil, 'tis well to know what to choose.

LOCATION OF THE GARDEN.—If it is to be a family garden, designed primarily to furnish an all-season supply of fresh things for the home table, the location should be one handy to the house, but not handy to the hen-house.

If it is to be a truck garden, primarily for profit, nearness to a city or fair-sized town is an important point to consider. Why? Because market, manure and labor will then be within easy reach, and the gardener can more easily keep posted on market conditions. Long hauls are expensive; long-distance connections are not always satisfactory. If he can not locate within easy driving distance of such a place, then the next best thing is to choose a spot within easy reach of railway station or steamboat wharf, whereby quick transportation (preferably

without transfers) may be had direct to a good
market. And, in either case, let him beware of bad
or hilly roads over which he must pass to reach market or transportation line. Hauling big loads up
hill or through mud or over ruts and stones is—
well, it isn't good business.

SLOPE, AND WIND PROTECTION.—I agree with R. L.
Watts, when he says: For the production of *early*
vegetables, the aspect or exposure is an important
factor. Earlier truck can be produced on land with
a southern or southeastern exposure. Locations not
naturally protected by hills or woodland may be
made warmer by the planting of hedges for wind-
breaks. The Norway spruce is excellent for this
purpose. It is particularly important to have the
coldframe and hotbed plat well protected from the
north and west winds.

As TO SOIL.—Any soil, he states, which produces
satisfactory crops of wheat, corn and oats, will generally give good results when planted with vegetables. Some vegetables, however, require special
peculiarities of soil and do not thrive when planted
in soils wanting in such properties. For example, it is
impossible to grow first-class carrots, salsify, radishes
and other vegetables with long roots, in a soil containing much clay. These and many other vegetables
thrive best in sandy soils, while cabbage, cauliflower
and sweet corn prefer heavier soils. Sandy soils produce the earliest and smoothest vegetables, and such
soils are very easily tilled, yet they are extremely
leachy and require liberal applications of manure to
maintain productiveness. Distinctly gravelly soils,
containing very little clay, should be avoided. Heavy,
stiff tenacious clays are not desirable for any branch
of gardening, although quite susceptible to perma-

nent improvement. Reclaimed bogs and swamps are excellent, when properly handled, for the production of onions, celery, etc.

W. W. Rawson, in his well-known book on market gardening, says: "Sandy loam, with a sandy or gravelly subsoil, should be selected. A clay subsoil, at least until underdrained, will render any land cold, as it retains the moisture."

DRAINAGE.—To do this subject justice would require more space than I have at my disposal. Suffice it to say that most garden soils can be greatly benefited by a system of underground tile drains, and, also, that some soils are absolutely unfit for garden purposes until they are underdrained. Tile drains help to make wet soils drier, and dry soils more moist. Write to the U. S. Department of Agriculture, Washington, D. C., and ask for a copy of free Farmers' Bulletin No. 187, entitled, Drainage of Land.

PLANNING AND LAYING-OUT.—Begin this preliminary work early. Study the characteristics of your land, its wet and dry places, its sandy or clayey spots, etc. Measure it accurately. Then figure out, on paper, a definite planting plan, showing just where everything should go, the distance between rows, and ideas about successional plantings. The diagram of a garden, pictured in this chapter, may give you some useful hints. It is a plan drawn by John W. Lloyd for an Illinois Experiment Station bulletin. No distances between rows are given in this reproduction of his plan, for distances would depend upon whether the garden is to be worked by hand or by horse power. (The correct distances for planting are given, either way, elsewhere in this book.)

EAST

NORTH

HORSE RADISH

(WATERMELONS)

PERENNIAL ONIONS

RHUBARB

(MUSKMELONS)

ASPARAGUS

{SUMMER SQUASH}

{WINTER SQUASH}

(CUCUMBERS)

(EGG PLANT)

(PEPPERS)

(LATE BEETS)

EARLY CABBAGE

(PEAS-FOLLOWED BY LATE CABBAGE)

(EARLY BEETS)

ONION SETS

(PARSNIPS)

(PEAS-FOLLOWED BY CELERY)

(SECOND EARLY CABBAGE)

(LETTUCE)

(PEAS-FOLLOWED BY LATE CAULIFLOWER)

(LATE SWEET CORN)

EARLY SWEET CORN

(EARLY CAULIFLOWER)

(EARLY TURNIPS)

ONIONS

(PARSLEY)

(TOMATOES)

STRING BEANS

LATE CARROTS

(PEAS-FOLLOWED BY TURNIPS, ETC)

(EARLY POTATOES-FOLLOWED BY TURNIPS ETC)

(SPINACH)

(BUSH LIMA BEANS)

(PEAS-FOLLOWED BY STRING BEANS)

EARLY CARROTS

(SALSIFY)

18 17 16 15 14 13 12 11 10 9 8 7 6 5 4 3 2 1

DIAGRAM OF A GARDEN—MERELY A SUGGESTION—CHANGE IT TO SUIT YOUR OWN NEEDS

Whatever plan you decide on, endeavor, if possible, to have *long, straight rows,* which will permit much of the work to be done by wheel hoe or by horse power. Therefore, run the rows the long way of the garden or field; whether the rows run north and south or east and west is not so important. Plan to have level rows, not elevated little beds divided into squares by paths. Let the spaces between rows be the paths, generally speaking. Some folks seem to think that a garden must be a series of beds raised higher than the path or ground level; this, in most cases, is a great mistake, for such elevated places soon dry out and the plants suffer for moisture. If the ground is naturally so damp that raising the beds is necessary to "get them up out of the wet," then the practise may, perhaps, have the shadow of an excuse—but 'twould be much better to underdrain ground which is so wet.

THE MARKET GARDEN.—The capital and equipment required for a successful commercial venture in trucking, vary according to localities and circumstances, but the average is much higher than most people suppose. The late Peter Henderson, a very successful gardener, estimated that three hundred dollars per acre was needed for equipment (tools, implements, horses, wagons, glass, frames, etc.) and for working capital (rent, labor, manure, fertilizer, marketing expenses, etc.). This would not include the purchase of land or buildings, and the estimate is based on an area of ten acres or less.

W. W. Rawson, in Market Gardening, says: "The amount of capital required varies with the amount of land cultivated, but not in proportion. While it might require about three thousand dollars, with the labor of three men and two horses, properly to handle two acres, I estimate that there would be needed about five thousand dollars, six men and three horses, for ten acres."

The foregoing estimates are based on the best, most intensive, culture, with many hotbeds and cold-frames, near New York and Boston, where the rent or cost of land is high. On cheaper land in some other localities, or on land farther away from cities, the capital requirements should be less. Under such conditions, perhaps five hundred dollars capital would suffice, if a careful, experienced man had five acres of good land paid for. Or even considerably less than this amount, if he had a general farm and raised a few acres of truck merely as a side issue.

As to Profits.—Well, they depend so much upon circumstances, seasons, localities and the *man,* that general estimates are apt to be misleading. From one hundred to three hundred dollars per acre, net, is perhaps a fair average. H. S. Weber, of Pennsylvania, recently figured his year's profit on a patch of about seven acres, as follows: Fertilizer, seed, hired help, marketing expenses, etc., $394; gross receipts, $1,700; net profit, $1,306, or about $186 per acre.

The Home Garden.—By this I mean the "kitchen garden," which is intended to furnish an ample supply of fresh or canned goodies "all the year 'round."

A ONE-HORSE PLOW WILL DO IF SOIL IS LIGHT AND AREA NOT TOO LARGE

Here the conditions are quite different from the foregoing. The area to be worked is smaller, the labor and expense less, and the market is right at home — sure and reliable. Here the spade or digging fork (I prefer the latter) often takes the place of the plow, the rake doubtless performs the duty of a harrow, elbow grease may be substituted for horse power, and hand hoes, hand planters and seeders, hand cultivators, weeders, diggers, sprayers, etc., are often substituted for horse-drawn machinery. Fertilizers are applied to square rods or square feet instead of to acres, and manure is perhaps hauled in wheelbarrows and spread by hand instead of in a machine manure-spreader. And the results are just as good—often better—than those achieved by the commercial gardener. Many times, too, a surplus is grown, which can be sold for good hard cash.

Does it pay? I say, *Yes!* So does ·Harriet. Tim echoes the sentiment, and Martha echoes Tim. Here's what Chas. C. Woodruff, of Illinois, said in Farm Journal: "I have a small town garden, 28 x 30 feet—just 840 square feet—and I take care of it without help, except that I hire it spaded in the spring. I am a printer, and it is necessary for me to be at the shop from 7 A. M. to 6 P. M., and the time I have for gardening is before and after these hours. I have kept an account of seeds bought, and the amount the produce would have sold for on the market at the time of gathering. Seeds, labor, etc., figure up exactly $3.95, and cash value of produce exactly $55.29. Think of it!—fifty-five dollars' worth of produce from an outlay of $3.95. Then the recreation! I got about $200 worth of that, with about $500 worth of satisfaction thrown in. Fifty-five dollars' worth of produce raised on 840 square feet of ground is at the rate of $2,488 worth of produce per acre. On most of my ground I raised three crops. No room for weeds. The work was healthful recreation; far better than loafing down town, and better pay."

I have seen the statement that an area 100 x 150 feet should furnish an ample supply of vegetables (exclusive of winter potatoes) for an ordinary family. So it should But let me say right here that s m a l l e r p a t c h e s than that

SPRING HARROWING SHOULD FOL-
LOW PLOWING AS SOON AS
POSSIBLE

often produce enough for average needs. Intensive culture will accomplish wonders on even a tiny plat.

PLOWING.—The time to plow depends upon circumstances. Early spring is the usual time, although fall-plowing has advantages when the ground is soddy or badly infested with wireworms, cutworms, grubs, etc. How deep to plow? As deep as you can without bringing up much of the subsoil. (Subsoil plowing requires a separate plowing with a special kind of a plow designed to loosen up the lower strata without bringing it to the surface; few gardeners, however, go to this extra trouble and expense, if they have a deep, mellow, well-drained soil. But subsoiling frequently pays. It need not be done oftener than once in two years.)

Never work soil when it is very wet and sticky; wait until it dries into crumbly, workable condition.

TRENCHING AND RIDGING.—To trench a strip of ground means to throw off the topsoil, spade up the subsoil, and then replace the topsoil. It's a great

deal of work, and not always so necessary as some of the old-fashioned books taught. For hard, shallow soils, or for deep-rooting crops like carrots, etc., it certainly brings good results. Subsoiling is the same thing, practically, but it's done with a plow, and is therefore easier in large gardens.

AFTER HARROWING, SMOOTH THE GROUND. THIS IS ONE WAY TO DO IT

Ridging land usually means to fall-plow it into ridges or beds, so that depressions ("dead furrows") occur, say, about every ten feet. Surface water then runs into the furrows, allowing the ridges to dry off more rapidly, permitting of earlier working in the spring. Properly drained or tiled land seldom requires ridging. (Ridging or hilling or banking celery, etc., is a different operation.)

A GOOD LAND-ROLLER
COMPACTS AND SMOOTHS

FERTILIZING AND MANURING.—See Chapter IV.

HARROWING. — The Acme harrow is a very good general-purpose smoothing harrow. The spring-tooth harrow is helpful on rough, stony, uneven land. The spike-tooth, or peg-tooth, is a splendid all-round harrow (but it should be so made that the teeth can be given a backward slant when it is desired to work recently-planted potatoes or corn). Harrowing should follow plowing as soon as possible in the spring, and be very thorough—lengthwise, crosswise and diagonally, until the ground is as fine and mellow as an ash heap. The disc harrow is an excellent implement for spring work on fall-plowed ground, and for other special purposes.

PLANK DRAG, OR ROLLER. — After harrowing, smooth or "float" the ground with some kind of a home-made drag, or roll it with a field roller.

A HOME-MADE PLANK
DRAG FOR SMOOTHING
LAND

(See several illustrations in this chapter.) Then the soil should be in compact, excellent condition for marking and planting, for which see Chapter III.

DIGGING TOMATO PLANTS. THIS GARDENER STARTED SEED **IN** THE HOTBED SOIL ; FLATS ARE OFTEN MORE CONVENIENT

CHAPTER II

HOTBEDS AND COLDFRAMES

Seeds, like mankind, are able to sleep well and get up early, if they have a good bed.—Tim.

HOTBEDS should be located near an outbuilding which can be warmed and used for transplanting work. It is also an advantage to have them near the water supply, unless the water is piped to the beds. A southern aspect is desirable and the frames should run east and west, with the glass sloping to the south, says R. L. Watts.

The pit for the hotbed should be dug in the fall before the ground is frozen. It is not necessary in Pennsylvania to excavate to a greater depth than about two feet four inches. The pit should be six feet wide and long enough to accommodate the number of sash to be used. It should be lined with heavy boards, preferably chestnut, nailed to chestnut or locust stakes. If the ground is level, the frame should extend twelve inches above the surface of the soil on the upper side and six inches on the lower side. This will provide for the proper drainage of water from the sash. In making the frame, it is best to have two or three sash at

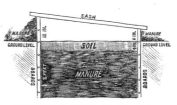

SECTIONAL VIEW OF HOTBED

hand, so that no mistake will be made in the measurements. Cross-bars or sash supports, 2 x 3 inches, are placed three feet apart where each two sash meet. Locate the hotbed in a well-drained spot.

Fresh horse-manure, containing a liberal amount of straw or other litter, is the best material to furnish heat in the hotbed. If manure is saved from the home stable, it should be collected and preserved under cover. It requires about one two-horse load for every two sash. When sufficient manure has been saved, or procured from livery stables, tramp compactly into piles about five feet square and three feet high. In three or four days, or less, considerable heat will be generated by fermentation, and the manure should be tramped into another pile, throwing the outer portions into the center of the pile. When fermentation is well under way in the second pile, throw the manure into the pit in successive layers, tramping continuously. Fill the pit to within four or five inches of the top of the frame on the south side. The manure will settle several inches before time for sowing the seed. Place sash on the frame immediately after filling, and plunge a thermometer in the heating material so that the bulb is four inches below the surface. The heat will rise rapidly until it reaches a temperature of, at least, 120°. A high temperature may be maintained for a week or more, but it will not do to sow seed over such hot material. Wait until the temperature drops below 90°, then place two or three inches of good soil over the manure if flats are to be used (see Chapter III), or about four inches if the seed is to be sown directly in the soil.

COLDFRAMES.—Coldframes are u s u a l l y constructed in the same manner as hotbeds except that they are simply built on top of the ground and no manure is used, heat being furnished by the rays of the sun.

SASH FOR HOTBEDS AND COLDFRAMES.—It is more convenient to use sash which are not very large, continues R. L. Watts. We have in use four hundred 3 x 6 foot sash, and we believe a larger size would be of no advantage, but rather a disadvantage. Our preference for thickness is one and three-eighths inches. The best material is cypress or cedar. If quite a number of sash are to be used, it is more economical to do the glazing at home. Paint the

sash before glazing, using a liberal supply of oil in the white lead. After the paint is dry, the glazing may be begun. It is best to procure single-strength A glass rather than cheaper grades. There should be three runs of 10 x 12 glass, each run requiring

THE HOTBED SHOULD BE SHEL-
TERED FROM COLD WINDS BY
WALL, FENCE OR WINDBREAK

six panes, or eighteen panes per sash. Overlap the panes about one-fourth inch. Secure the glass at each lap by the smallest-sized glazing points. After driving in the points, apply putty or mastica. After this hardens, paint the sash again.

FIRE HOTBEDS.—In some sections nearly all the market gardeners use fire hotbeds, says E. R. Jin-nette. It is neither difficult nor expensive to make a fire bed. The bed is warmed by two flues extending from the fire-box or furnace. In clay soils the flues are often simply trenches cut in the soil six or eight inches deep, the width of a spade at the bottom and eight or ten inches at the top. They are covered with flat stones. Six-inch drain tiles make good flues. The furnace can be made of stone or brick. It should be two feet wide, two feet high and four feet long. Old grate-bars, or a section of an old boiler, make a fine top for the furnace. Fire beds vary in length from fifty to 200 feet, but seventy-five to 100 feet will prove most satisfactory. To insure a good draft the flues must have a rise of three or four feet to the 100 feet of length. For this reason it is better to make the bed on a gentle south slope. Start the bed eight or ten feet from the furnace. The earth on the flues next to the furnace should be at least three feet deep, tapering down to four or five inches at the upper end. It is best to have the bed extend east and west, and the flue on the south side should be within six inches of the edge of the bed. That on the north side can be a foot or more from the edge. At the fire-box the top of the flues should be on a level with the top of the furnace, and both flues should open into chimneys at the upper end. To save fuel the furnace should have a door.

GREENHOUSES.—The construction and operation of greenhouses heated by the hot-water system, is

VENTILATION MUST BE CARE-
FULLY REGULATED, OR GLASS
REMOVED ON WARM DAYS

hardly a subject within the scope of this little book; those who are interested in the matter need a special volume—such as Prof. Bailey's, The Forcing Book. Few gardeners can afford to build greenhouses unless they are operating on a very large scale, in which case they will find it cheaper and easier to furnish heat by fuel in the furnace than by manure in the hotbed. The air of the hotbed is liable to become very damp, as well as too hot, and these two conditions may cause serious trouble by the "damping off" of plants. When the weather is cold and the winds severe, it is difficult properly to ventilate hotbeds without chilling the plants. All of the points are in favor of the greenhouse.

GLASS POINTS

A hotbed, after the heat is spent, can be used as a coldframe, if desired.

The outside of the hotbed frame should be banked with manure. This helps to keep in the heat.

A properly made hotbed is good for six or seven or sometimes eight weeks; the heat gradually declines.

If the hotbed manure is loose and fluffy after being trodden, there is too much straw in it; if it packs soggy and solid under the foot, there is too little straw. It should feel springy when trodden, but should not swell up quickly in a loose mass when released from pressure.

The coldframe is used for: 1. Growing some of the vegetables and flowers late in the fall, such as lettuce, radishes, violets, etc. 2. Receiving plants which have been started earlier in hotbeds and forcing houses, to harden them for outdoor planting. 3. Wintering hardy plants, such as cabbage and lettuce and all plants which can be sown in the fall. 4. Growing lettuce, radishes, celery plants for late setting, or anything which is planted or needed later than hotbed stuff.

"With thirty-six sash for coldframes, and a small greenhouse 16 x 24, we raised 18,000 cabbage plants, 5,000 tomato plants, some eggplants, peppers and lettuce plants, and 20,000 sweet potato sprouts," writes H. S. Weber, of Pennsylvania. "We found a ready market for the plants; cabbage at $5 per thousand, tomatoes at $10 per thousand and sweet potatoes at $2 per thousand. The eggplant and peppers sold at fifteen cents per dozen. In addition to the foregoing, we raised enough for our own use."

DRILLING SEED. ROWS WOULD BE STRAIGHTER IF LINE HAD BEEN
USED FOR FIRST ROW

CHAPTER III

SOWING AND PLANTING

Oh, bend your back and sow the seed,
For the glad spring days are here,
And he who labors has little need
Of the harvest time to fear.

I N the production of early tomatoes, peppers, eggplant, celery, cabbage, etc., it is very important to have strong, thrifty plants ready for the field the first day it is safe to transplant. A delay of a few days may be the cause of reaching the market too late to catch the highest prices.

TESTING SEEDS.—The strength and vigor of a plant is largely dependent upon the character of the seed used, says Pennsylvania Bulletin No. 147. Old seeds are generally slower to germinate, and frequently produce weak plants. It is, as a rule, safer to use new seed, and it is also important to procure large, plump seeds. To avoid trouble and disappointment, it is desirable to purchase seed not later than January 1st, and to test carefully before making the main sowing. In the absence of hotbeds at that season of the year, and if no greenhouse is available, the test can be made in the kitchen window. Count two lots of one hundred seeds of each variety to be grown, sow in separate rows in a shallow box, and count the plants that come up. This is a more certain and practical test than by sprouting the seeds between damp cloths. At least seventy per cent. of the seeds should sprout vigorously.

STARTING THE HOTBED PLANTS.—Preparation should be made the previous fall by storing away soil to be used in starting the plants. Good garden or field loam, or compost, as free as possible from weed seeds, should be selected for this work. Loams in which there is little or no clay are the best, as such soils will not bake to any considerable extent.

If a greenhouse is available, it is best to sow in drills on the bench soil. If a hotbed is to be used, it is more convenient to sow in drills in shallow plant boxes (called "flats"). After filling the boxes, press the soil firmly, especially in the corners and along the sides. With a narrow straight-edge, such as a piece of plastering lath, make furrows (drills) about two inches apart and one-fourth to three-eighths of an inch deep. The seed may be sown broadcast, covering one-fourth inch, but the preference is to sow in drills. The plants come up better and are more convenient to lift at the time of transplanting. After sowing, cover the seed or close the furrows, firm the soil with a wooden block, and water thoroughly. The watering may be done either before or after setting the flats in the hotbed.

Beginners are often perplexed as to how thick to sow the seed. This matter can be better regulated by sowing in drills than when broadcasting. A flat the size of an ordinary soap-box is large enough to grow seven or eight hundred plants, or even more when there are no mishaps. In sowing cabbage, lettuce, pepper, tomato, eggplant, etc., from twelve to fifteen seeds per each inch of furrow is about right. If the furrows are of uniform length, the seeds may be counted for one furrow, and a small measure devised (as a thimble partly filled with paraffin) to sow about the same quantity of seed in each furrow. After sowing the seed the furrows can be filled rapidly by moving a straight-edge over the ridges. If the seedlings seem to crowd too much when they grow, thin them out as soon as possible, press the soil about the remaining plants, and then water enough to settle the ground.

VENTILATION, MOISTURE, ETC.—Heat and moisture must be carefully regulated and controlled. A high temperature and excessive moisture, with little ventilation, necessarily produce weak, spindling plants. Every possible effort should be made to maintain a moderate temperature (not above 90° nor below 60°) in the greenhouse or hotbed, and it is important not to water more than is absolutely necessary. In the management of hotbeds, ventilation should be attended to daily; water only when the ground looks dry. Warm the water in cold weather to avoid chilling plants. For time of sowing see chapters on the different vegetables.

TRANSPLANTING TO HOT OR COLD FRAMES.—In about four weeks the seedlings are usually ready to transplant. By that time the fourth or rough leaves will be formed and a good root system developed. Whether the plants should be transplanted to hot or to cold frames depends upon the variety, the time and the season. Hardy plants like cabbage, cauliflower, lettuce, etc., may go into coldframes early, but tender plants such as tomatoes, peppers, eggplant, etc., should not go into coldframes until the time and weather make such a change safe; these last are sometimes moved early to hotbeds and then later to coldframes. Fill flats with a mixture of about half well-rotted manure and half soil, and the addition of some bone meal. A thin layer of fine soil is placed on top, making each flat level full and soil quite firm. The flat is now ready to plant.

The transplanting board, see illustration, is placed over the flat, resting on a box or table of con-

R. L. WATTS' TRANSPLANTING
BOARD AND DIBBER,
ON "FLAT"

venient h e i g h t. (This transplanting board can easily be made of sound lumber, cleated at the ends with strips. The board s h o u l d be large enough to cover the flat, as shown. Holes are bored at the required distances with a three-quarter-inch bit. For cabbage, tomato, lettuce and most other plants the holes should be about two inches apart for the first transplanting. Of course, the holes can be made with an ordinary stick or dibber, and without the aid of this board; but the board is certainly a help when many plants are grown.) Place the left hand on the board, holding it firmly, and with the right hand and special-shaped dibber (the dibber should work freely), punch the holes in the soil ready to receive the plants. If the soil contains just the right amount of moisture (which can be regulated by sprinkling and mixing before placing board on top of the flat), no trouble will be encountered in making the holes or in transplanting. One boy will punch the holes as fast as six or eight can plant. Boys drop a plant in each hole, and a man can fasten roots very rapidly. If the soil contains the proper amount of moisture, little or no watering is necessary immediately after transplanting.

When these flats are placed in the frames very

little or no ventilation is given until the plants are established, which, under favorable conditions, requires only two or three days. It is best to keep a humid atmosphere until new roots are formed, and this can not be accomplished if ventilation is too free. If the sun is very hot, which may be the case in the spring when tomatoes and peppers are transplanted, the frames should be shaded with straw mats, turning back the edges of the mats six to twelve inches to admit light and sunshine. Look the flats over daily and water only the dry spots. After the plants have made a good start, admit air and keep soil moist. Close the sash toward evening, before the air gets too cool; and if the weather is quite cold, place mats on the frames not later than four o'clock in the afternoon. Remove mats early in the morning, if the weather permits; and, when there is no danger of freezing, the mats should not be put on the frame until as late as possible in the evening.

The plants of cabbage, lettuce and cauliflower should be *well* hardened before setting in the field. After they have reached the proper size, give them all the air they will stand. When the plants have had a few days of free exposure to the air by removing the sash, leave off the mats for two or three nights, and then do not cover with sash at night. If the process of hardening is gradual, the plants named may finally be frozen stiff in the frames without damage, and, after freezing in the frame, they will stand almost any amount of hard freezing in the field. Of course, tender plants, such as tomatoes, peppers, eggplant, etc., must not be frozen in the hardening process.

ADVANTAGES OF FLATS.—Plants are frequently raised by sowing seed in the soil placed directly on the manure in the hotbed, then transplanting into rich soil in another hotbed or coldframe. Although this method is employed successfully by many gardeners, experience has taught that it is more convenient and satisfactory (unless a greenhouse is available) to sow the seed in flats or shallow plant boxes, transplanting into the same kind of boxes. The weather is often very severe at the time the seed should be sown in the hotbed, but if flats are used, the work may be done in a warm outbuilding; water them there if more convenient, and then place the boxes in the hotbed. When the time for transplanting arrives, the flats of plants may be carried to a warm room provided with tables or benches, and the work of transplanting to other flats done with ease and comfort. It is often cold, wet and disagreeable when early plants should be transplanted into the frames, and it would be quite impossible to work advantageously in the open air under such unfavorable conditions. When flats are used, a large number may be planted, set back on the floor or shelves, and, if the weather is cold, the planted flats can be hurried to the frames where they may be quickly covered with the sash. Also, when the plants are ready for the garden or field, the flats can be watered thoroughly, loaded on a wagon and hauled to the field, where they can be distributed at convenient intervals. By standing flats on end and jarring lightly, the compost will separate from the bottom and sides of the flat, and the hand can be slipped under the layer and plants removed by breaking the compost which has become a network of fine roots, thus taking out each plant with considerable compost attached to the roots. This is a most important matter in transplanting early vegetable plants. When all the foregoing advantages are considered, it seems that no one should attempt to grow early vegetable plants in quantity without the use of flats. It is an advantage to have the flats uniform in size and of such dimensions that no space is lost in the hotbeds or coldframes. Make them of, say, half-inch wood of any kind. They should be two or three inches deep, and not too large to handle easily when filled.

DIRT-BANDS FOR MELONS, ETC.—Dirt-bands are very convenient for starting melons, cucumbers, squashes and lima beans in hotbeds. They are each made of a thin strip of wood veneering eighteen inches long and three inches wide, grooved so as to fold up into a bottomless box four inches square and three inches deep. They are placed in the hotbed without tacking. Pressing them down into the dirt will hold them in shape until they are filled with soil. They can be taken out of the bed four at a time with a spade, placed on the wagon or sled, and the spade slipped from under them. In the field they can be taken from the wagon with a spade. If properly wet down before removal from the bed, and handled carefully throughout, very little dirt will fall out of the boxes in transplanting, and, therefore, the roots will not be disturbed. Hundreds of thousands of dirt-bands are used by the truckers of southern Illinois, and most dealers in box material carry them in stock early in the season. They cost from $1.00 to $1.25 per thousand. The bands can be used, after removal from around the plants, to protect them from the hot sun.

Three-inch paper pots are sometimes used instead of dirt-bands; some gardeners like to transplant tomatoes, etc., in them. They are made of stout paper, and may last several seasons. (Of course, my readers will understand that pots, dirt-bands, or similar ideas, are only *necessary* in the case of plants that are difficult to transplant in the ordinary way. Tomato, cabbage, etc., will endure considerable root disturbance and rough handling; but melons, etc., will not.)

GROWING PLANTS UNDER CLOTH.—In some parts of the South, truckers are able to grow many early vegetables, etc., with only the slight protection afforded by cotton cloth, stretched over wooden frames. This, in a very mild climate, can perhaps take the place of glass for some purposes. In a North Carolina state bulletin, however, W. F. Massey discourages the idea that cloth is cheaper to use than glass in that state. He says: "Cloth is, in the long run, far more expensive than glass; also, when the difference between the crops is considered, it is the more costly from the start, because of the less profit that can be had from it; and in severe spells it is almost out of the question to prevent serious damage, which would not be the case with glass-covered frames." (Some extensive southern growers get around the latter danger by installing a steam or hot-water outfit, and running pipes through a long series of cloth-covered frames.—J. B.)

MATS TO PROTECT FRAMES.—The cold nights would be destructive to the plants if given no other protection than the sash. Some gardeners rely mainly on wooden shutters, but these are not so warm as mats, and can not be placed on the frames nor be removed so rapidly. Mats of various materials, such as burlap or rubber cloth packed with cotton or waste material, have been placed on the market by dealers, but some gardeners make mats from rye straw, which are just as serviceable at must less cost.

They can be made on rainy days, or through the winter when the gardener is usually not very busy. Each mat should be 6 x 6½ feet in size, so that it will cover two sash in width, and allow the extra half-foot to lap over the ends of the sash at top and bottom.

MARKING THE GROUND OUTDOORS.—Many growers plant with a line stretched across the patch and moved into place for the next row; this insures absolutely straight rows (for which I have a great liking), but is not well adapted to large fields. In very small gardens a long, straight board can be laid down, and the planting done along its edge. On large areas, however, it is very convenient and time-saving to mark out the entire field in advance of planting. For this purpose there are several styles of home-made

HOME-MADE ONE-HORSE MARKER

markers, one pulled by horse power, and another kind drawn (backward) by hand (see illustration on this page). By making a few changes, these markers are easily adjusted to any width of row desired.

If deep markings are wanted—that is, if a man wants furrows instead of mere guide marks—a one-horse plow, or a cultivator rigged as a furrower, can be used by following the shallow marks previously made by a marker. Or a three or four row horse furrower can be made at home, similar to the one pictured on the next page.

HOME-MADE MARKER WITH SEVEN ADJUSTABLE SLEDS

It requires a steady

horse, a good eye and practise to make fairly-straight marks or furrows. It is a great help to stretch a line as a guide for the first furrows across the side of a field; then, coming back, keep one outside

marker tooth or sled in the inside mark made during the first trip; and so on, till the field is finished. (The furrower operator in the picture is practising this very thing, but he neglected to stretch a line

A HOME-MADE THREE-ROW FURROWER

for the first or outside rows, and, therefore, his furrows are not so exact as they might be.)

PLANTING DISTANCES.—In the various chapters on vegetables, etc., will be found hints regarding how far apart to plant the different varieties.

TRANSPLANTING TO THE FIELD.—The method of doing this with flats has already been mentioned. If plants have been grown directly in the soil in frames, then, of course, they must be dug (without disturbing the roots more than is necessary), placed in boxes convenient for handling, hauled to the field, kept moist and out of the sun, and planted as rapidly as possible. E. R. Jinnette says: "Instead of using flats, my way is to soak the soil in the frames with water. Then with knife or spade cut the soil into blocks—a plant in center of each—and take blocks up with a spade and move them on wagon to field." As soon as the field is planted, start the culti-

vator, and make a nice "dust mulch" to conserve
moisture. The best times to do transplanting are
before a rain, or toward evening.

It is often a help to shade the newly-set plants
for a few days, but this is hardly practicable in a
large field; the small grower, however, can utilize
shingles, newspapers, berry boxes, etc., etc., for this
worthy purpose. Here's a simple little device that
may be of help to some of my gar-
den friends: Take some stout paper
(tar paper is good), cut it in the
form illustrated, fold it together and
tack on the seam to a light stick;
then adjust the "hood" over a newly-
set plant. A hundred hoods can be made quickly
and cheaply.

DIBBERS, ETC., FOR TRANSPLANTING.—The transplanting tool used by many gardeners is a short,
pointed stick, called a "dibber" or "dibble," and having a handle of any convenient shape. L. H. Bailey,
in his book, Principles of Vegetable Gardening, says:
"In the working hand hold the dibber; in the other
hand hold the plant; the plant is lowered into a hole
made by the dibber (which makes a hole but does
not remove the earth). (The earth is best closed
about the plant by inserting the dibber alongside of
it, an inch or so distant, and then giving the handle
a quick push toward the plant—thus pushing soil
into the first hole while the plant is held in place with
the other hand.) It is customary to have a boy
carry the plants in a covered basket or box, and to
drop them just ahead of the planters. One boy ordinarily will drop for two rows of planters; he should
not drop faster than the plants are required. Set
the plants deep. Gardeners usually prefer to set

them to the seed-leaf, even though they were an inch
or two higher than this in the original seedbed. This

THREE KINDS OF
DIBBERS

deep planting holds the plants in
position and places the roots in
the moist and cool earth. Press
the earth firmly about the roots
and crown; this is very important. If the ground and season
are very dry, have the boy follow with a pail and put a dipper-
ful of water about each plant.
After the water soaks away, the
dry loose earth should be drawn
about the plant to afford a surface mulch. In larger
operations a tank on wheels is drawn through the
fields * * * Transplanting machines drawn by horses
are now becoming popular for large-area practise,
and these are supplied with a watering device * * *
A quick man can transplant from 5,000 to 6,000 plants
in a day, if the soil is light and in good condition.
Ten acres of cabbage plants sometimes may be set
in a day by means of a horse machine."

Other tools besides dibbers and horse machines
are often used in transplanting. For instance, strawberry plants are frequently set with a spade; and
many gardeners mark out deep furrows for tomatoes,
etc., put manure and fertilizer where plants are to
go, mix it with the soil, and then set the plants with
the aid of a spade, trowel or hoe, and a boy or man
to carry the plants and hold them in place. (A picture in Chapter XIV shows how this method of
fertilizing tomatoes is done.)

After the plants are set, always start the hoe or
cultivator and level the ground nicely.

OUTDOOR SOWING OF SEEDS.—Now we have gotten

away from plant-setting, and will consider the sowing of seeds in drills or hills in the open ground.
What has already been said about marking and fur-
rowing, applies here, too—if you wish to drop seed
by hand. The furrower will do for potatoes, peas,
etc., and the marker for other crops. (Cover the
furrows, after sowing, with a hoe or a one-horse
plow; or rig your cultivator with side shovels—taking off the back and front teeth—so that it will
throw the dirt into the furrow from both sides.)
Fine seeds may be sown in hills, shallow drills
or marks, and covered with a hand hoe or a wheel
hoe.

The easiest and nicest way to sow small seeds,
however, is to use a machine planter, seeder or drill.
There are very excellent and inexpensive hand drills
or seeders made, that will sow almost any kind of
seed in continuous drills, or drop seed at regular
intervals of one, two, or several, inches apart—according to the way you set the machinery. These
machines open and cover the furrow, can be regulated to sow seed plentifully or sparingly, and the
hill-dropping feature saves seed and considerable
after-thinning in the rows. There is a hand-power
onion-seeder now on the market that sows the seeds
at the right distance apart, *two rows at a time*—
thus saving much thinning and half the walking and
time. There are hand corn-planters, hand potato-
planters, machine corn or potato-planters pulled by
horses, and, in fact, handy planters and sowers for
every purpose. Most of these drills and machines
have a marker which marks the next row; thus, if
you get the first row straight with a line, the others
will correspond (see full-page illustration facing beginning of this chapter). Always test the drill on a

board or barn floor, and regulate it to drop correctly before using it in the field.

VARIETIES TO PLANT.—Every locality has its favorite varieties. In a general book, such as mine, it is not feasible to give long lists of varieties; the best I can do is to mention, in the different chapters about vegetables, etc., a few standard varieties that do well almost anywhere. Write to your state experiment station and ask for a list of varieties best suited to local climate and soil. As for new kinds— "novelties"—go slow. Try a few in a small way each season, but don't discard the time-tested varieties until a novelty is proved to be better.

TIME TO SOW.—This varies, of course, in the different sections of the country. Consult the chapters about vegetables, etc., where approximate dates suited to the latitude of Pennsylvania are given. Allow about five days' difference for each 100 miles north or south of this latitude.

ROTATION OF CROPS.—Supposing that you were a radish or a melon and had to grow up every summer in the same spot in the same little field, eat the same food, and fight the same old bugs and fungous diseases year after year—well, wouldn't you get tired and stunted and hungry for a change of air, scene and food? Of course! Then don't forget to change the location of the different crops each season. Follow corn with potatoes, or beets, or something else, but don't follow corn with corn, or potatoes with potatoes. Systematic rotation of crops is a great help in the fight against insects and fungi.

"Puddling" means to dip the roots of dug plants in thin mud, preliminary to transplanting into the open field. In very dry weather this process helps to keep the roots from drying.

E. R. Jinnette, of Illinois, and many other market gardeners, say that it is quite important to cut or "shear off" the top one-third or one-half of the leaves of celery, cabbage, etc., before transplanting to the open field.

SPROUTS

Nothing but experience can teach the air requirements of plants in hotbeds or coldframes. Watch the thermometer, the sun, and the wind's direction, and raise or lower or take off the sash accordingly.

"I do not use a hotbed," says H. E. Haydock, a successful New York State gardener. "I find that a number of shallow boxes in a sunny room answer every purpose in starting the tomatoes, cucumbers, melons, etc., that I intend to raise."

A wide, iron garden rake and three or four pieces of corn-cob make an easily-constructed garden marker. Wide or narrow spaces may be marked at will, by changing the cobs. (See cut.)

Soaking seeds of slow germination, as the beet, parsnip, carrot, etc., is practised sometimes with good results. With the proper seedbed, however, soaking is seldom necessary, especially if the ground is thoroughly "firmed" after planting. This may be done with the feet, the back of a hoe, or by rolling, and is a very important operation.

There is a new kind of a sash on the market, with double glass—making an air-space between top and bottom panes. Plants under such sash would not easily freeze during moderate cold-snaps, even if no mats were used. An air-space, however small, is an excellent non-conductor of either cold or heat; but of course double glass is not so cheap as single.

Many gardeners on a small scale do not care to bother with growing plants in hotbeds and coldframes, and so buy such plants ready-grown. This is often the cheapest way when only a few dozen tomato, cabbage, celery, pepper and similar plants are needed for setting outdoors. Varieties of vegetables that are not usually transplanted (such as carrots, corn, potatoes, etc.) of course need no preliminary hotbed or coldframe growth.

Don't blame the seedsman if you sow tender things, like peppers, tomatoes, etc., too early in hotbeds with insufficient heat, and then find that most of the seeds rot. Nor do not blame him if seeds sown outdoors rot because the soil is too cold or wet; nor because insufficient moisture in the ground fails to cause germination. Buy the best seed and place your order early.

Hardiness of Vegetables: Beans, melons, cucumbers, corn, tomatoes, squash, pumpkins, sweet potatoes, eggplant, peppers and okra are all very "tender" and easily harmed by a slight frost; they should not be set outdoors in the North until the weather is warm and settled. Other vegetables, properly handled, will endure more or less frost and cold, and are therefore called "hardy." Some of the latter, however, are more hardy than others—onions and peas are especially proof against cold.

The seeds of some vegetables possess greater vitality than others. The pioneer gardener, Peter Henderson, claimed that peas, beans, peppers, carrots, corn, eggplant, okra, salsify, thyme, sage and rhubarb are safe for only about two years; asparagus, endive, lettuce, parsley, spinach and radish are safe for about three years; broccoli, cauliflower, cabbage, celery and turnip are safe for perhaps five years, while the beet, cucumber, melon, pumpkin, squash and tomato may retain their vitality for six years or more.

Three important objects are gained by transplanting to coldframes before setting in the field: The plants are hardened or accustomed to a lower temperature; and, second, their roots are toughened by the move, and so suffer less when the final move is made to the open field; and, third, they are given, in the coldframe, more room to grow wide and stocky. Growers who want extra-large, stocky tomato plants, etc., sometimes transplant them several times, each time giving them more space in the frames.

"In field culture, the most important matter in the germination of seeds is the supply of moisture," says an expert. "Satisfactory germination can not be secured with an insufficient amount of soil moisture. Thorough preparation of the ground is essential. It is also necessary to *firm the soil* after sowing, drilling or planting. A firm seedbed, bringing the seed into intimate contact with moist soil, is the secret of quick germination, provided the ground is warm and the depth of covering not too great. The proper depth depends upon the variety." (See chapters about vegetables, etc.)

Plant labels are often wanted in the garden, but as ordinarily made are usually soon rendered unreadable by the action of rain and sun. Seedsmen sell excellent and durable metal labels, but they are not very cheap. Here's a good idea from Prairie Farmer: Cut two pieces of lath (as shown in the illustration), and fasten together at top with one tiny clinched nail—so that the short piece of protecting cover will swing. Only the part to be written on need be smooth. The name may be written in pencil, or the printed name from the seed envelope may be glued on. The labels may be used many seasons, gluing fresh names over, or erasing and rewriting.

Here's a method of raising flower plants, melons, etc., in the house for transplanting outdoors, without the expense

of buying pots. Take old fruit cans and unsolder them in the fire. Tie the tins together with a stout string, and set them on a board (see picture). Fill with earth and plant seeds. When ready to transplant, cut the string, and the earth with its mass of roots can be lifted and set in a hole in the ground, without disturbing the roots in the least degree. The tin, of course, flies open when the string is cut. (Some gardeners start early melons, etc., indoors on inverted thick pieces of sod.)

Usually it is cheaper and better to buy seed than to attempt to grow and save it. Sometimes, however, there are advantages in home saving, and many successful gardeners produce at least one or two kinds of seed at home. But unless a man is making a specialty of something, and is located in a place where its seeds are at their best, I doubt the advantage of home-grown seed. Good seed means careful yearly selection; good judgment; knowledge of the variety; a systematic discarding or "roguing" of undesirable specimens; and an ideal type in mind, toward which the strain is constantly pushed. Remember that the tendency of improved kinds of plants is to deteriorate or revert to early types, and only a careful annual selection and "weeding out" can prevent a backward tendency. Plants, like animals, may be "bred up," but it requires patience and skill to do it. If you plant little potatoes every year, or select inferior tomatoes for seed, or have seed melons where squash pollen can mix with them, good results are not likely to be attained. Keep most seeds that you save in a mouse-proof, insect-proof tin box in a dry place; seed corn on the ear should be hung up by the husks, in the attic; seed potatoes need to be kept in a dark, cold cellar, or stored in an outdoor pit.

THE WHEEL HOE IS USUALLY SENT FORWARD WITH A SERIES OF LITTLE, QUICK PUSHES; DO NOT TRY
TO FORCE IT STEADILY ALONG EXCEPT PERHAPS IN VERY SOFT SOIL.

CHAPTER IV

FERTILIZATION. CULTIVATION. IRRIGATION.

Spare the weeds and spoil the crop;
Stint the food and growth will stop.

THERE are many kinds of fertilizing materials, and all are useful in some way and in some degree; only experience and observation can show which are best for *your* soil and *your* crops. In a general way, however, I will say that there is no better all-purpose fertilizer than stable manure—all you can get of it, say from ten to twenty tons to the acre. Haul it on the ground in winter and early spring, and spread it as it is hauled; plow it under, and then broadcast (to each acre) about 400 pounds of kainit (a commercial form of potash), and about 600 pounds of finely ground bone meal; harrow this in, and you have a very good, complete mixture which contains all essential elements of plant food. Or, if you desire, you can substitute muriate or sulphate of potash for the kainit, or twenty-five bushels of unleached hardwood ashes; or phosphates or superphosphates may be substituted for the bone.

If stable manure can not be obtained, and if there is sufficient humus in the soil, buy a high-grade, complete, ready-mixed, commercial fertilizer—the best you can get, not the cheapest—and broadcast it on plowed land at the rate of about 1,200 pounds to the acre (more or less according to the soil and the crop). Or, if you care to bother with the home mixing of such a fertilizer, you can buy the separate ingredients, mix them yourself, and perhaps save some money. Write to the U. S. Department of Agriculture, Washington, D. C., and ask for free Farmers' Bulletins Nos. 44, 192, 245, 257 and 278, and you will obtain full information on this and kindred subjects.

HUMUS.—This has to do with the mechanical condition of the soil. Humus is decayed vegetable matter, without which any soil is almost worthless. Humus separates the soil particles, makes the ground mellow and loose, and aids it to retain moisture and air. A soil without humus is dead, airless, and either dry and hard as a stone, or a sticky mass of mud. Therefore, stable manure has a value aside from its fertilizing contents—i. e., its ability to supply humus to the soil. Leaves, straw, or any decaying vegetation, would answer the same purpose. If these things can not be had, then the gardener must occasionally grow some crop like clover, rye, vetch, oats, etc., which can be plowed under and thus furnish the necessary humus.

COVER CROPS.—By these are meant humus-making crops which are sown broadcast after vegetables, etc., are off, and which then grow through the fall, cover and protect the ground through the winter, and are plowed under in the spring in time for regular garden planting. Red clover, or sand vetch, or rye, or oats and crimson clover combined, etc., may be used for this purpose. A "catch crop" is the same as a cover crop, only it is sown at the last cultivation, before the vegetables are off.

NITROGENOUS CROPS.—Nitrogen is the most expensive of all fertilizing elements, but if the gardener can not afford to buy enough of it (in stable manure or nitrate of soda, etc.) he can supplement his supply by producing it right at home. How? By the simple process of growing some crop which has the ability to extract nitrogen from the air and store it up in the form of nodules or lumps on its roots. Plants of this kind are called "legumes"; the principal ones are: Clover, vetch, beans, peas and cowpeas. Any one of these, if planted as a cover crop or as a crop to plow under, adds nitrogen to the soil and greatly improves the land. This process is called "green manuring," and if the garden is not full of humus and if stable manure can not be had to supply nitrogen cheaply, it may pay you to spend a preliminary season in the growing and turning under of such crops—supplementing the nitrogen thus obtained by broadcast applications of potash and bone meal in the spring, and lime in the fall. (NOTE: Oats, rye, etc., furnish humus but no nitrogen; legumes furnish *both*.)

NITRATE OF SODA.—Much is heard about the quick results produced by this nitrogenous fertilizer, but unless it is handled with great carefulness I can not recommend its use. Harriet says that it is "more like a stimulant than a food." It must be applied in small doses often. Yes, and with care—or you'll kill your plants. About 100 pounds at a dose to the acre is usually enough, and, generally speaking, it should not come in direct contact with plants. (Nitrogen may also be purchased in the form of dried blood, guano, tankage, cotton seed meal, sulphate of ammonia, etc.)

LIQUID MANURE.—This, like nitrate of soda, is a

quick stimulant (but usually a safe one in this case). I. M. Angell, New York State, contributes the following experience: "A satisfactory plan for supplying the manure water, was to set a large perforated tin pail into a rack that was fastened across the top of an ordinary wash-tub. A spigot was fitted into the wash-tub near the bottom. Whenever liquid manure was required, a quantity of manure from the stable was placed in the tin pail and enough water poured through it to fill the wash-tub into which it drained. By turning the spigot we drew off into a pail whatever we wished to carry to the plants. This 'filter' has been in use several seasons and is entirely satisfactory. The manure is rich enough to supply a number of tubfuls of the mixture before it is necessary to replace it. To apply the liquid manure we turned up a furrow with the hand plow, close to the row, poured in the water, and turned back the soil with the same tool. This method puts the liquid where it will do the most good, and the loose earth that is returned to its place makes the best sort of mulch; and by the same operation the ground receives cultivation. Nitrate of soda may be used in the same way on such a garden. Our method is to mix one pound with enough water to wet 100 feet of row. By the time the garden has all received a share, perhaps in the course of several days, the first vegetables treated will be ready for another dose."

LIME.—Some soils are "sour." Lime will correct this acidity and sweeten things generally, besides helping to unlock and make available the stores of fertility which may be in the ground. Applied to stiff clay soils, it renders them loose and friable; while it binds together sandy soils, thus making them more retentive of moisture and fertility. Take fresh stone lime, slack it with water until it becomes a dry powder, then broadcast it in fall or early spring and work it into the soil. The quantity to apply per acre varies from twenty to forty or more bushels. Farmers' Bulletin No. 77, U. S. Department of Agriculture, Washington, D. C., explains this matter fully. Better get a copy. Harriet has mine safely filed away in the desk in my room, and I shouldn't like to spare it.

COMPOSTS.—For flower pots, small gardens, hotbeds, coldframes, window gardens, etc., a well-made compost is very useful. It is simply a mixture of ordinary soil with well-rotted sods, stable manure, leaves, or any other available vegetable matter. Pile the various ingredients in a long, low pile outdoors and fork it over several times at intervals, thus fining and mixing all thoroughly together and hastening decomposition. A little freshly-slaked lime added to the mass is an advantage. The pile may be started in the fall, or whenever desired, and should be ready for use in six months or a year (according to materials used). Some gardeners put potato and tomato vines, etc., on the compost pile—any waste stuff, in fact—but if there are any blights or fungous diseases in the garden, 'twould be safer to burn such vine and plant refuse than to use it in a compost and thus spread the trouble.

CULTIVATION.—The offices of tillage are several. Among the more important ones are:

1. The setting free of plant food by increasing the chemical activities in the soil.

2. The soil is made finer and hence presents greater surfaces to the roots, thus increasing the area from which the roots can absorb nutriment.

3. The surface of the soil is kept in such condi-

tion that it immediately absorbs all the rain that falls during the summer, when it is apt to be dry. Little is lost by surface drainage.

4. Moisture is conserved thereby. Where the surface remains undisturbed for weeks the soil becomes packed, so that the moisture from below readily passes to the surface and is evaporated, thus being lost to the growing crop. If the surface is kept light and loose by tillage, so that the capillarity is broken, but little of the soil moisture comes to the surface and evaporation is not so great. In this way nearly all the moisture remains in the soil, where it can be used by the roots.

5. Thorough tillage has a tendency to cause deeper rooting of the roots. The surface of the soil is made drier by tillage during the early part of the season than it would otherwise be; hence the roots go where the soil is moist. The advantage of deep rooting during drought is obvious.

6. Weeds and grass are kept out—and we all know the importance of this.

MULCHING.—There are two kinds of mulch—the "dust mulch" caused by regular surface cultivation, and the mulch which is applied in the form of straw, leaves, stable manure, or similar materials. For nearly all purposes I prefer and use the "dust mulch." The main object of mulching during the growing season is to prevent the evaporation of moisture in the soil, and shallow cultivation does that effectively; and does not, like other forms of mulch, furnish breeding places for insects and fungi. In special instances, however, a mulch of litter is a good thing. For instance: Straw, etc., will keep strawberries clean in a fruiting bed; currant bushes root so near the surface that ordinary cultivation often injures the roots, and therefore a light working of the soil in spring followed by a heavy mulch of stable manure, etc., is an excellent plan to follow; in the fall a mulch of strawy manure, etc., protects and fertilizes the roots of vines, plants, bushes, etc., during cold weather, and prevents the alternate freezing and thawing which causes plants to "heave" out of the ground more or less.

IMPLEMENTS FOR CULTIVATION.—For a small garden I should choose a medium-sized, ordinary-shaped hand hoe; a single-wheel hoe and its various attachments of tiny rakes, cultivator teeth, plows, etc.; one wide, iron hand rake (say about sixteen teeth), and a narrow one with not more than eight teeth; and one or two of the claw-like hand weeders here illustrated. In addition I should buy an extra hand hoe and cut it with a file into the shape shown by

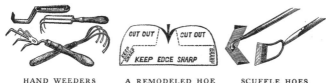

HAND WEEDERS   A REMODELED HOE   SCUFFLE HOES

the dotted lines in the accompanying picture; this kind of a hoe is very useful at times, especially in the strawberry patch. The narrow rake mentioned, can, in mellow ground, often be used easier and to better advantage than any hoe.

Some gardeners prefer one style of wheel hoe, some another; there are several good makes on the market and the amateur can not go far astray if he buys any one of them. But I should not advise the purchase of the combinations of seeder and wheel

THE ONE-HORSE CULTIVATOR IS THE THING
FOR MEDIUM-SIZED AREAS

hoe, etc., which are on the market; buy your seed planter separately. A wheel hoe, if rightly used, is a great labor-saver; but do not think that you can push one steadily along like a horse cultivator — it should be sent forward with a series of little, quick pushes, an inch or so at a time. The single-wheel hoe is mostly used for work between rows; the double-wheel hoe is especially adapted for straddling and working on both sides of a row. Of the two styles, for ordinary use, I personally prefer the single wheel—it is lighter, cheaper to buy, and easier to operate; but many truckers and onion growers prefer the double wheel for large areas.

For the larger garden, or commercial truck field, I should want an assortment of hoes of different shapes and sizes, a double-wheel hoe, a good one-horse cultivator for working between two rows, and (if the area were large enough) a two-horse cultivator for working two rows at once.

ON SMALL AREAS THE HAND
WHEEL HOE TAKES THE
PLACE OF A HORSE
CULTIVATOR

There are various makes of good cultivators on the market. I own three kinds, each adapted to one horse: An iron-frame, adjustabl e-wheel, five-tooth cultivator; a twelve-tooth machine; and one with five spring-teeth. All have their uses and all are adjustable to depth and width. The first mentioned implement has several attachments — side "shovels," side "sweeps," rear "hoes," etc.—which are often helpful for special needs; the flat, wide, surface-skimming sweep attachments are particularly good for killing such weeds as thistles, which are apt to dodge and escape the ordinary cultivator tooth.

FOR LARGE AREAS THE TWO-HORSE CULTIVATOR IS SOMETIMES BEST

THINNING PLANTS.—This often necessary work must be done by hand early, when the seedlings are quite small. To get a sure "stand" of plants it is usual to sow more seeds in the hill or to put them closer together in the row than is advisable for the plants' later good, and then to thin or pull or cut out the surplus plants when the stand is assured. The distance apart to thin depends upon the variety; for hints on distances, consult the chapters on vegetables.

IRRIGATION.—In regions of normal rainfall, artificial watering of gardens is seldom practised or necessary. Cultivation, under normal conditions, conserves sufficient moisture for the average plant's needs. In California and some other states, irrigation is a necessity. Folks who need to practise this method should write to the U. S. Department of Agriculture, Washington, D. C., and ask for free

Farmers' Bulletins Nos. 46, 116, 138, 158 and 263. 'Twould be impossible, here, to give full information on this subject. But a few general hints are in order: If you must water plants, etc., or if the season is so abnormally dry that regular rainfall and cultivation does not suffice, remember that one good *soaking* is worth many surface sprinklings. Endeavor to apply the water toward evening, and cultivate (or mulch) the surface as soon as possible

DIFFERENT KINDS OF HOES ON A HANDY
NOTCHED RACK

the next day. If the water supply is limited (and it usually is), do not apply it to the surface but in furrows opened alongside the plants (as directed under head of. Liquid Manure in this chapter), then, when the water has soaked in, cultivate the soil back into place. Do not sprinkle water on plants when the sun is shining hot. Don't think that you can irrigate a big field with an ordinary wind-mill outfit—it takes a tremendous quantity of water to soak even one acre.

HINTS FROM EXPERIENCE

Sharp hoes make short work. Carry a file and apply it often. Learn to use a hoe so as to leave the ground *smooth*. Keep hoes clean.

Do not mix lime with fertilizers, nor wood ashes with hen manure. Why? Because the valuable ammonia (a form of nitrogen) would thus be set loose and would escape.

Hen manure is good for the garden, but it is very strong and should not be applied too freely nor in contact with the roots. In fact, all fertilizers and manures should be well mixed with the soil, so that it will not hurt the roots.

The important thing in any garden is not to allow the weeds to get a *start*. They are easily kept down when young by stirring the soil, but once allowed to gain headway, the labor of fighting them is greatly increased. Weeds kill easiest when the sun shines hot.

Stable manure is not a perfectly-balanced ration for plants, because it contains rather too much nitrogen and not quite enough of the other essentials. Therefore it should be "balanced" by the addition of potash and phosphoric acid (as advised in the forepart of this chapter).

A "complete" fertilizer must contain these three ingredients: Nitrogen, phosphoric acid, potash. A well-balanced commercial mixture suitable for average garden purposes should analyze about as follows: Nitrogen, four per cent.; phosphoric acid, eight per cent.; potash, ten per cent.

Market gardeners sometimes use a special form of a hoe called a "scuffle" hoe. It derives its name from the way it is scuffled or shuffled back and forth close to the surface, doing quick work in killing weeds and leaving an even surface. But it is not adapted to loosening up the soil.

The advised quantities of fertilizers per acre mentioned in this chapter aren't of much help to a reader who has only a small garden patch. So here's a rule to help him to figure out the matter to meet his own requirements: 1,000 pounds to the acre is six and one-quarter pounds to each square rod.

It is generally best to practise shallow cultivation. I usually set my horse cultivator to run about two inches deep; this plan best conserves moisture, and avoids all danger of cutting roots. Once in ten days is not too often to cultivate; and always, after a rain, the ground should be stirred with cultivator, rake or hoe as soon as dry enough to work.

Several times in this chapter I have referred to "broadcasting" fertilizers. This can be done by hand with a shovel, or by the aid of a machine fertilizer spreader. Better yet, the fertilizer can be drilled in with an ordinary grain drill or with a special fertilizer drill—thus requiring no "harrowing in" afterward. Some gardeners find that it is more economical to apply fertilizers and manure *only to the row or the hill;* this plan certainly saves fertilizer, but it requires more fuss and work.

It is an easy matter to determine whether a soil needs lime. Five cents will buy at a drug store enough blue litmus paper to test a large field. Cut the paper into narrow strips and make tests in different parts of the field by pressing the moist soil into close contact with the paper. If the paper turns red in a few minutes, a sour soil is indicated and lime should be applied. The degree of acidity will be shown by the extent to which the blue paper turns to red. A growth of sorrel is often an indication of a sour soil. The plowing under of heavy green crops usually causes sourness and necessitates applications of lime.

Guiding a horse cultivator: Some folks have difficulty in the double duty of holding the handles and managing the reins. A steady, slow-walking horse is required, and you'll need to buckle or tie on an extension to the length of ordinary lines. To operate, buckle or tie the lines together, put them around the upper part of your body beneath both arms, and have the lines just long enough to be gently taut as you hold to the cultivator handles and walk along. Thus adjusted, a slight twist of the body either way will guide the horse to right or left as may be required; and at the end of the row a touch on the lines with the hand will "gee" or "haw" him around for the return trip. Soon he'll learn the work and keep his proper place almost automatically. If at first he walks too fast, lean back steadily on the lines until he learns a slower pace. Always cultivate each aisle between two rows, *twice*—up on one side and back on the other; keeping the same order in each aisle, so that the horse will learn which side to walk on. Few people can do good work by cultivating through an aisle just once and trying to watch both rows.

IRRIGATION !

CHAPTER V

SPRAYING. FORMULAS. GARDEN PESTS AND FRIENDS.

Many a man who imagines he could conquer the world and all the folks in it, can't even manage the pests in the garden.—Dorothy Tucker.

PRAYING mixtures are divided into two classes: Fungicides and insecticides. Often, however, I find that it is practicable to unite the two into one spray—and thus fight both fungus and insects at the one operation. A mixture of Bordeaux solution and an arsenical poison, is a good example of such a combination. Bordeaux mixture is the best and most useful of all known fungicides for general use.

FUNGICIDES.—Bordeaux mixture is made by taking four pounds of sulphate of copper, four pounds of quicklime, fifty gallons of water. First, dissolve the copper sulphate. The easiest, quickest way to do this, is to put it into a coarse cloth bag and suspend the bag in a receptacle partly filled with water. Next, slake the lime in a tub, and strain the milk of lime thus obtained into another receptacle. Now get someone to help you, and, with buckets, *simultaneously* pour the two liquids into the spraying barrel or tank. Lastly, add sufficient water to make fifty gallons. 'Tis safe to use this full-strength Bordeaux on almost all foliage—except, perhaps, on extra-tender things such as watermelon vines, peach trees, etc. For these it is wiser to use the following half-strength mixture: Two pounds of copper sulphate, two pounds of quicklime, fifty gallons of water.

Formalin: This is also called formaldehyde, and may be purchased at drug stores. Its principal use in the garden is to treat seed potatoes to prevent a fungous disease of the tubers called "scab." Soak the whole seed for two hours in a mixture of one-half pint of formalin and fifteen gallons of cold water; dry the seed, cut, and plant in ground that has not recently grown potatoes.

Powdered sulphur: For mildew on rose leaves, gooseberry bushes, etc. Dust or blow it on when the plants are wet.

BORDEAUX COMBINED WITH INSECT POISON.—By adding one-quarter pound of Paris green to each fifty gallons of either of the Bordeaux formulas, the mixture becomes a combined fungicide *and* insecticide. Or, instead of Paris green, add about two pounds of arsenate of lead (an excellent commercial form of this, called "Disparene," is for sale by seedsmen). The advantages of arsenate of lead over Paris green are, first, it is not apt to burn foliage even if used in rather excessive quantities; and, second, it "sticks" to the foliage, etc., better and longer.

INSECTICIDES.—Sometimes I find it desirable to apply a treatment for insects alone, without the bother of making the regulation Bordeaux. Here are a few standard formulas suited for chewing insects:

Paris green: Two pounds of quicklime, one-quarter pound of Paris green, fifty gallons of water. The lime helps to neutralize the caustic action of Paris green on tender foliage; potato vines are so tough, however, that in their case the lime may be omitted, if desired. Keep mixture well agitated while spraying. (Not so safe as arsenate of lead on very tender foliage.)

Arsenate of lead: This can be made at home, as follows: Take twelve ounces of acetate of lead, four ounces of arsenate of soda, and fifty gallons of water. Put the acetate of lead into a gallon of water in a wooden pail; in another wooden pail put the arsenate of soda in two quarts of water. When both are dissolved, pour them together into the spray tank containing the required amount of water. A white precipitate of lead arsenate immediately forms in the tank and the mixture is ready to be applied. This remains in suspension longer than Paris green. The ready-prepared commercial form called "Disparene" simply needs dissolving in water—about two pounds to fifty gallons of water. (For rose-bugs use ten pounds.)

White hellebore: This, if fresh, may be used instead of Paris green in some cases—worms on currant and gooseberry bushes, for instance. (It is not such a powerful poison as the arsenites, and would not do so well for tough insects such as potato bugs.) Dissolve one ounce in three gallons of water, and use as a spray.

For Sucking Insects.—Now we come to another class of insecticides, suited to insects which suck a plant's juices but do not chew. Arsenic will not kill such pests; therefore we must resort to solutions which kill by *contact*. Here are some of the best-known recipes of this kind:

Kerosene emulsion: One-half pound of hard or one quart of soft soap; kerosene, two gallons; boiling soft water, one gallon. If hard soap is used, slice it fine and dissolve in water by boiling; add the boiling solution (away from the fire) to the kerosene, and stir or violently churn for from five to eight minutes, until the mixture assumes a creamy consistency. If a spray pump is at hand, pump the mixture back upon itself with considerable force for about five minutes. Keep this as a stock. It must be further diluted with soft water before using. One part of emulsion to fifteen parts of water is about right for lice.

Carbolic-acid emulsion: This is made by dissolving one pound of hard soap or one quart of soft soap in a gallon of boiling water, to which one pint of *crude* carbolic acid is added, the whole being stirred into an emulsion. One part of this is added to about thirty-five parts of water and poured around the bases of the plants, about four ounces per plant at each application, beginning when the plants are set out and repeated every week or ten days until the last of May. To bring about the best results, some of the earth should be removed from about the plants before pouring on the emulsion. Used to fight maggots in the soil.

Whale-oil soap solution: Dissolve one pound of whale-oil soap in a gallon of hot water, and dilute with about six gallons of cold water. This is a good application for aphis (lice), and scale on house plants, lilacs, etc.

Tobacco tea: This solution may be prepared by placing five pounds of tobacco stems in a water-tight vessel, and then covering them with three gallons of hot water. Allow to stand several hours;

dilute the liquor by adding about seven gallons of water. Strain and apply. Good for lice on peas, roses, etc.

Buhach: This is also known as pyrethrum, or Persian insect powder. The best is called California buhach; the imported powder is not so fresh as a rule and therefore not so strong. It may be used as a dry powder, dusted on with a powder bellows when the plants are wet; or one ounce of it may be dissolved in three gallons of water, and sprayed on the plants at any time. It is often used on flowers, in greenhouses, on vegetables, etc. Although a contact poison, it can in some cases be used instead of the more dangerous arsenites—on cabbages, for instance, to kill the cabbage worm.

Fir-tree oil: An effective remedy against mealy bug, red spider, thrip, green fly, etc., on household plants, and in greenhouses, etc. Seedsmen sell it, and directions for use accompany it.

SPRAY PUMPS, ETC.—A good spraying outfit is an essential part of a gardener's requirements. The kind of an outfit to buy depends, of course, on the size of your garden and the plants to be sprayed. If you have only a small patch a few square rods in size, perhaps a cheap hand atomizer (see picture) will answer the purpose. These hold a quart of liquid, and

HAND ATOMIZER FOR SMALL GARDENS

seedsmen and implement dealers sell them for about 75 cents if made of tin; brass, about $1.25.

A large powder-bellows for applying buhach, sulphur, etc., outdoors, costs about $3.00—smaller sizes for indoor use are cheaper. (A less satisfac-

tory but often-used method of applying the powder,
is to punch numerous small
holes in the bottom of a small
tin pail, fill with the powder,
and then shake it over the
plants when they are wet.)

POWDER BELLOWS

If the garden is more than a "small patch," and
yet not too large, doubtless one of the new-style,
compressed-air, shoulder-strap sprayers (sold by
seedsmen and implement dealers) will answer the
purpose (see illustration).

A COMPRESSED-AIR SHOULDER-
STRAP SPRAYER. (NOTE SPE-
CIAL ATTACHMENT FOR
REACHING UNDER-SIDE
OF LEAVES)

Or, if the area is ex-
tensive, you may require
a barrel or tank outfit,
mounted on the farm
wagon and worked by
hand; or perhaps your
requirements may ne-
cessitate one of the
power outfits which are
operated by either a
gasoline engine, geared
connection with wagon
wheels, or compressed
gas in cylinders; some
of these outfits are ar-
ranged to spray several
rows of potatoes, straw-
berries, etc., at once (a
four-row automatic
sprayer is illustrated in this chapter on page 61).

Before deciding upon a pump, or buying one,
take a bit of the same advice that was given in my
Orchard Book: "Write to advertisers in the Farm
Journal or other farm papers, get their catalogs

and price lists, and then study and compare, and decide which suits your purpose best."

A good pump should work easily, maintain a steady spray from one or several nozzles, be simple in construction, have non-corrosive brass working parts, be durable and able to stand hard use, be easily taken to pieces for repair, have pipes properly arranged to prevent clogging, and be provided with an agitator which keeps the solution in vigorous

A FOUR-ROW COMPRESSED-AIR MACHINE
FOR LARGE AREAS

motion and thoroughly distributed. Judging a pump by cheapness alone is likely to be poor economy.

Nozzles: The Vermorel nozzle is very popular; so are several other makes that I have tried. The main thing to demand is a nozzle that will throw a fine mist, like steam, which settles on the plants like dew. A sprinkler, resulting in much "drip" upon the ground, is not wanted. And, too, a good nozzle should not clog easily, and when it does clog it should be quickly cleanable. (NOTE: All spraying mixtures should be strained before using, to prevent clogging the nozzles. A box, with the bottom and top knocked out, will make a frame for a strainer; a brass-wire mesh—eighteen or twenty meshes to the inch—can be securely tacked around the bottom to complete the job.)

HINTS

Never spray strawberries, etc., when they are in blossom.

Fungicides are not cures, but *preventives*.   Therefore, such spraying should begin early in the season.

Poultry: Harriet says that hens do not belong in all the garden, nor all the garden in the hens.   Either fence in the garden *or* the biddies.

Ants: These do no real harm in the garden; when found on plants or trees they are after lice.   Ant nests in lawns or walks may be destroyed with hot water, bisulphide of carbon, or kerosene.

Earthworms or angleworms: As a rule these well-known wrigglers do good rather than harm.   They loosen and aerate the soil.   Applications of lime will drive them away if they prove to be a nuisance in any special instance.

Rabbits, groundhogs, etc.:   In some localities, bunny is a decided menace to the garden.   He likes a nibble of this or that, and he's always hungry.   The same applies to Mr. Groundhog and some other animals.   A good preventive is a wire-netting fence, with the lower part sunk a foot beneath the soil; another is a good dog, or a gun.   Groundhogs can be killed by putting bisulphide of carbon in their burrows and stopping up the entrances.

Bisulphide of carbon: This is used to kill maggots, etc., in the soil, weevils in beans and peas, etc.   It comes in liquid form and may be had of druggists.   When exposed to the air it quickly vaporizes into a poisonous and explosive gas which is heavier than air and which will destroy all insect or animal life.   Its various uses are mentioned in several places in this book.   Caution: Do not inhale much of the vapor, and allow no lights near.   'Tis a safe and useful remedy only when properly used.

Snails: I have never, myself, had any trouble with these, but in some places they are said to be a pest. T. Greiner in his How to Make the Garden Pay, gives the following remedy: "Set traps by scattering pieces of orange peel over the ground.   Snails are so fond of this delicacy that they will remain clinging to the peel rather than go back to their hiding places at break of day.   Examine the traps every morning, and destroy the marauders."   With the aid of a lantern they can often be found and killed at night.

Moles and field mice: These little animals burrow underground and make small, irregular ridges in lawn or garden. They often "follow a row" with great exactness, and therefore some people suppose that moles prey on plant roots, seed, grain, etc.   As a matter of fact the mole is after grubs and insects that *are* feeding on the roots, and, therefore, he is—in this respect alone—doing the gardener a favor. (Experts once captured and killed a number of moles, to test the matter of their diet; only insects were found in their stomachs.)   But, unfortunately, Mr. Mole, in his quest for plant enemies, heaves up the ground, disturbs and breaks plant roots, and upsets things generally.   So the gardener declares him a nuisance.   The remedy?   One or two mole traps (sold by seedsmen and implement dealers), set in the mole's regular runways.   Field mice sometimes do injury to growing crops, and moles are perhaps blamed for it.   Remedies: Traps, cats, poisoned bait, or the "Ratite" virus sold by the Pasteur Vaccine Co., New York City.

Birds: English sparrows are often a pest in the garden, eating tender shoots, leaves, etc.   A few loads of fine shot fired at them occasionally will frighten them away.   If you live in town where you can not fire a gun, no easy remedy can be suggested.   Poisoned grain will kill them, but on account of the danger to pet animals and beneficial birds, I can not advise its use.   Cheap mosquito netting might be spread over a small patch; or around currant bushes.   I know of one strawberry lover who screens in quite a fair-sized bed of strawberries to keep robins, etc., from eating the ripening fruit; he uses wire poultry-netting, supported, top and sides, six feet high, and leaves the netting there permanently.   Crows and blackbirds frequently pull up planted corn, and pigeons are fond of peas, etc.   Scarecrows are of little use.   The best preventive is to tar the seed, as follows: Put the seed into a pail and pour on enough warm water to cover it.   Add a teaspoonful of coal tar to a peck, and stir well.   Throw the seed out on a sieve or in a basket to drain, and then stir in a few handfuls of

SCARECROWS ARE OF LITTLE USE

land plaster (gypsum), or air-slaked lime.   Do not pour the tar on the dry seed.   (In this place let me say that nearly all birds are beneficial to the garden in some way—crows eat field mice, and birds in general eat many insects that do harm.   Toads, also, are friends of the gardener, because of the many insects they devour.   Never kill or drive away a toad.   Lady-bugs or lady-birds are friends, too; they eat the tiny lice that suck a plant's juices.   Bees are beneficial, for they help the pollination of blossoms.)

CORRECT WAY TO USE AN ASPARAGUS KNIFE. BY PUSHING DOWN,
SLANTWISE, THE CUT IS MADE WITH LEAST
DANGER TO OTHER STALKS

CHAPTER VI

ASPARAGUS. RHUBARB. HORSERADISH.

Spring is almost at hand, but do not be too hasty to begin outdoor operations. Wait until the soil is sufficiently dry and warm. Nothing is gained by being in too great a rush.—Farmer Vincent.

SPARAGUS is a hardy perennial, which, when well started and cared for, should produce annual crops for twenty or more years. I have learned that the plants prefer a deep, well-enriched, loamy, moist but not wet, soil. Heavy clays are to be avoided; the ideal soil is a light, sandy loam. A sheltered spot with a sunny exposure helps to bring an early crop. Spade or plow the ground deeply. Many writers insist that trenching, two feet deep, is necessary, but very good results are obtained with a working of only about half that depth. Subsoiling after plowing is the ideal method for large fields.

For a small bed, the easiest way to get a quick start is to buy some one-year-old roots of a seedsman, and plant them in their permanent bed at once. One hundred roots, when well established, should furnish enough asparagus for the needs of an average family. Roots should be set, in the North, in very early spring; or they may be set in the fall, if well mulched. Farther south, of course, they can be set out in the fall or early winter. Make furrows six inches deep and three feet (four feet is better for horse cultiva-

tion) apart, and set the plants—crown up and roots
down and well spread out—about two feet apart, in
the bottom of the furrows. Cover three inches deep,
and when the shoots are up a few inches, work the
rest of the dirt into the furrows and level the ground.
(If all the covering is put on at once, the first shoots
may be too feeble to push through six inches of soil.)
When planting, expose the roots to sun and wind as
little as possible.

Let the plants grow at will the first season; simply keep the ground well cultivated and free from
weeds. Applications of salt are not really necessary,
although salt is helpful to keep down weeds. After
frost has killed the tops, mow them off close to the
ground and burn them; then apply a good mulch of
stable manure (bone meal and kainit may be added).
The second season, the same, except that two or
three early cuttings may be made before the stalks
are allowed to grow; but "go easy" on cutting, that
year, or you'll weaken the roots. The third (and
subsequent) seasons, work the ground lightly and
early, keep out weeds and asparagus seedlings, cut
every shoot clean and about three inches deep until
July 4th, then let the plants grow; cut off and burn
them after frost, stir the ground lightly and apply
manure, etc. (In the early spring the coarser portion of the mulch may be forked off, and the remainder lightly forked or cultivated in.)

Blanched asparagus: Some people and markets
demand "blanched" (whitened) shoots; these are no
better to eat, but have an attractive, distinctive appearance. Blanching is accomplished by ridging or
"hilling up" (plowing or throwing the soil toward)
the rows in the early spring before the shoots appear;
the shoots have to push through several inches of

extra soil and thus more of the underground or white part can be obtained when gathering. (NOTE: R. B. Handy says that if the lay of the land permits, it's an advantage to have ridged rows of asparagus run north and south, on account of better distribution of sunshine on both sides of the ridges when thus arranged.) Cutting is usually done with a special-shaped asparagus knife (see illustration) which facilitates very deep cutting. The blanched stalks are not usually allowed to get much above the surface, and cut-

AN ASPARAGUS "KNIFE" IS MORE LIKE A CHISEL

ting is done regularly every day, care being taken not to injure stalks not yet up, or the crowns. The aisles between four-foot rows may be cultivated regularly with a horse without hurting the hilled-up crop; and the ridges may be kept clean by light hoeing or raking, *after* cutting. Or a double harrow, composed of two sections hinged in the middle, and of sufficient width, may be used in two-horse form to work astride the ridges. After the cutting season is over the ridges should be plowed down and flat cultivation given until the growth of tops prevents. (This ridging or blanching method is quite common among market gardeners, but the level-culture method given in the foregoing paragraphs is often preferable for the small home-garden—and either method is better than the old way of growing asparagus in "beds.")

Marketing asparagus: An asparagus "buncher" (see picture) is a great help to me in getting bunches ready for sale.

AN ASPARAGUS BUNCHER IS HELPFUL

When cut off uniformly at the butts, washed, and tied with neat, narrow tape, or cord, they are ready for the customer or for packing into crates for shipment. Sizes of crates and bunches vary in different localities; usually the bunches are about four inches in diameter and seven to nine inches long. Asparagus is a profitable crop when properly handled. No other crop responds more generously to liberal and intelligent treatment. One of the most successful Illinois growers makes three grades, and the bunches of each grade are tied with different colored ribbon or tape. The stalks in each grade are uniform in size and quality. His entire crop is shipped to Chicago and handled by one firm. When cutting "grass," he is careful not to leave the stalks long in the sun after being cut. The yield to the acre varies greatly—from about 500 to 2,000 bunches, according to soil and season. The later crop can often be sold to canneries.

Growing asparagus from seed: This is easily done, and the gardener who wants many plants can save money by growing his own. Two ounces of seed should sow about 100 feet of drill; two pounds should grow enough roots to plant an acre. This seed germinates very slowly, and it is a help to soak the seed in warm water twenty-four hours before sowing. For wheel-hoe culture, make the rows about one foot apart; for horse cultivation, two and one-half feet apart. In the North, sow in early April; farther south, earlier, according to latitude. Cover the seed about an inch deep. When the plants are an inch or so high, thin them to about three inches apart. Give good culture all summer, and the next spring you should have some nice one-year-old roots to transplant to their permanent place. ('Tis said that one-year-old plants are more desirable for transplanting than two-year-olds; and that the male plants—those that bear no seeds—produce larger asparagus than the seed-bearing female plants; hence some few specialists go so far as to discard all seed-producing plants. If planted 2 x 3 feet apart, 7,260 roots are required for one acre; 2 x 4 feet, 5,445 roots.)

Another method: Mark out furrows, say four feet apart and six inches deep, on well-prepared, well-manured land. Sow the seed in the furrows and cover lightly. As the plants grow, gradually pull the soil to them until level, in the meantime thinning them out to about two feet apart. Perhaps the thinnings can be sold to a neighbor. Give careful cultivation, and your asparagus should be ready for business in two years. This method obviates the necessity of transplanting.

Asparagus is sometimes forced in hotbed, coldframe or cellar. Dig mature roots in the fall and store them until wanted. The roots, after forcing, are worthless.

Varieties of asparagus: Any variety is about as good as another; size and quality depend more upon culture and manure than upon the variety. Conover's Colossal, Palmetto, Barr's Mammoth and Columbian White are well-known kinds that I have tested.

Insects and diseases: The principal asparagus pests are beetles and rust. There are two kinds of asparagus beetles, both of which injure the plants by eating the green parts and making holes in the stalks, and by laying their eggs upon the plants, from which eggs grubs or larvæ hatch and feed upon the green parts of the plant. In habits, effects and remedies the two species are similar, but the beetles are different. Both species deposit rows of small dark eggs, placed endwise on the plants. The remedies for both are the same, and consist in regularly cutting low the entire patch of asparagus, thus destroying the beetles' food supply until July; or dusting with flour and buhach; or permitting a *portion* of the patch to remain uncut and spraying it with some arsenical poison, especially arsenate of lead, which will stick to the plants that are *not* to be used for food. Stalks covered with eggs may be cut down and burned at any time. Chickens and ducks, if allowed the run of the asparagus patch, will destroy hundreds of the pests. The ridged system is a help when beetles are plentiful, for blanched stalks are cut just as they peep through the ground, and so the beetle does not find much available material for eating or egg laying.

Asparagus rust is a fungous disease which most commonly occurs where the plants are too damp and the air circulation is poor. It is to be prevented by cutting all the plants low and frequently, and spraying with Bordeaux mixture during the season *after* the cutting stops. Cut and burn the rusty plants in the fall as soon as they ripen or commence to die. The disease is worse some seasons than others.

RHUBARB.—This, like asparagus, is a hardy perennial, and does best in a deep loamy soil made very rich with stable manure and fertilizers. In the small garden the rows may be about three feet apart; for horse cultivation, four feet apart. Space the plants about three feet apart in the rows, and set them deep enough to cover the top "eyes" about two inches. Except for large plantations I believe that it is best to buy the plants of a seedsman; set in very early spring; or in the fall, well mulched. An acre set 3 x 4 feet, requires 3,630 roots. No stalks should be pulled the first summer; a light crop the second season; a full crop the third.

Cultivation begins in the early spring and continues until fall, when a heavy coat of manure should be applied. Seed-stalks should be cut off whenever seen, so as to throw all the force of the plants into themselves. A plantation is good for about twenty years, but after a few years the roots develop into big "clumps" that need to be severely trimmed with a spade. Don't be afraid; cut straight down, all around; many of the trimmings can be used for new plantations or sold to neighbors. Each strong "eye," with roots attached, will, if removed and set in good soil, make a new plant; in fact, this is the common method of propagation. (Plants may be grown from seed, planted the same as asparagus, but this requires the loss of a year's time.)

Marketing rhubarb: Methods, markets and shipping-packages vary in different localities. Some Illinois growers begin pulling rhubarb as soon as the stalks are six or eight inches long, and ship in third-bushel climax baskets; they claim to get more out of it in this way. It is a question whether in the long run this is better than to let the stalks get full length before beginning to pull. Later on, the large, fifty-pound crate is often used. Whatever plan is adopted,

A LONG, LOW, WELL-BANKED SHED FOR FORCING RHUBARB IN WINTER

it is well to bear in mind that it does not pay to fill the packages with small stringy stalks, and top

them out with nice large ones. Better make two
grades, and pack honestly. See that the stalks are
large enough and that they are properly cleaned
and trimmed. In some markets the leaves may be
left on; in others they must be cut off. Some markets require bunching and tying; others do not. The
best-known varieties are: Linnæus and Victoria—
the former being the earlier kind. There are no insects or fungous diseases that are troublesome.

Forcing rhubarb: This is often done in the garden in a small way, by placing a barrel or tall box
(without top or bottom) over a strong clump of
"pieplant," and then banking up around it with
manure. Do this just before growth starts, and the
stalks will be ready to use much earlier than usual.
Matters may be hastened still more, I will add, by
placing a piece of glass over the top for a while or
during bad weather or cold nights. Or clumps of
rhubarb may be forced in an ordinary coldframe.

Rhubarb may be forced, commercially, in special
houses. Isaac Ridgeway of New Jersey does it as

PULLING OF RHUBARB BEGINS IN
MARCH IN THIS FORCING SHED

follows: He has a
long, low, well-banked
shed, plastered on the
inside and heated by
stoves (see illustra-
tions). Into this he
hauls and p l a n t s,
about December 1st,
frozen clumps of rhu-
barb. Fires are not
started, however, until
about the middle of
February. Pulling begins early in March, and is
done twice a week. He receives about five cents for

three stalks, and has sold as much as $1,500 worth from the building in one season. Stalks seem to grow all right in a dark place, and he says they sell for more than those grown under glass. (In a very small way, this forcing could be done in any ordinary cellar. It is important to let the clumps freeze before storing them inside.)

HORSERADISH.—The best soil is a rich, *deep,* loose, moist loam. This plant is a hardy perennial, says Prof. Bailey, in Garden-Making, but for market it is chiefly grown as an annual crop. "It is propagated by 'sets,' which are small roots (about the size of one's finger) which are trimmed from the large roots when the crop is stored in the fall. These sets should be cut in pieces four to six inches long, the top end square so as to mark the right end up—for if the sets are planted wrong end up, crooked roots will result. The sets are covered two or three inches deep in a vertical position. The roots are dug in late fall, and care is taken to get all the pieces of roots out of the land, for the plant is apt to become a bad weed. If old crowns are planted, crooked and branchy roots are obtained."

Sets made in the fall I tie in bundles and keep over winter packed in sand in a cool cellar. Rows should be about two and a half feet apart to permit of horse cultivation, or about half that distance for wheel-hoe work. Space sets about ten inches apart in the row.

DIGGING, TOPPING AND DRYING ONION SETS IN NEW JERSEY

CHAPTER VII

THE ONION

A certain amount of work in the garden is good for man—and also good for onions.—Harriet.

ONIONS like level, rich, black, moist land in perfect condition and with sufficient humus; however, any *good* soil will do; do not plant on rough, poor soil, nor on recently-turned sod. The crop is obtained in two ways— from seed and from "sets"; the result being either early "bunch" onions, or "picklers," or large onions, or sets for future planting, or seed to sell— according to how the crop is managed.

Nitrate of soda is particularly valuable in growing onions, says the writer of Farmers' Bulletin No. 39. One hundred pounds of nitrate per acre worked in before planting, and two or three dressings of about fifty pounds each during the season, will facilitate rapid growth and increase the yield if there is enough potash and phosphoric acid already in the soil. When onions are raised from seed sown where the crop is to mature, the drilling should be done as early as possible in the spring. Drills are made about half an inch deep and one foot apart for wheel-hoe cultivation (about two feet and a half for horse work). When plants are up, thin to two inches apart. Every other plant may then soon be pulled, bunched and sold in a green state; while the remaining plants may be left until maturity (if that is considered more profitable).

A common system of culture is to plant sets in the early spring instead of seed, and raise this vegetable to bunch for the early market. The ground can then be cleared and planted with a second crop of something else. If preferred, mature bulbs may be grown from the sets, and this method will insure success in almost any soil. Spring-planted sets should be covered about two inches deep, and spaced two to four inches apart in the row, the latter distance being best if you want large onions.

Another plan (called the "new onion culture") followed to a considerable extent in recent years, is to sow seeds of the large Spanish or Italian varieties, such as Prizetaker, etc., in the hotbed and then *transplant* into the field at the earliest possible date.

HAND-WEEDING IS A LABORIOUS BUT NECESSARY DETAIL

(These very l a r g e varieties need this early hotbed start to insure maturity in the short season of the North. Farther south they may be started in c o l d f r a m e s or sown in the fall outdoors.) This method is fully described in Farmers' Bulletin No. 39. Better get a copy.

A favorite plan with many gardeners is to plant sets about three inches deep outdoors in late August or early fall, using the Egyptian or winter varieties. This method insures a crop of green onions for bunching at the earliest possible date. (Onions are very hardy in the ground outdoors, but in the North it helps the fall-sown sets to mulch them when the ground freezes.)

The three most extensively grown of American onions produced from seed sown in the field are Yellow Danvers, Silver Skin and Red Weathersfield.

Still another method, sometimes practised in raising bunch onions for spring, is to sow the seed in the open ground in late September. In the North the rows may be protected by scattering a little mulch when the ground freezes.

A Systematic Business.—A while ago, Mr. B. F. Stetser, New Jersey, told in the Farm Journal how the onion business is conducted in his locality. His words are well worth repeating, so I'll give them here:

In early April the onion seed is sown in rows one foot apart. It grows until the middle of July, when the entire crop is gathered. The stalks are then about a foot high and the onions are about as large around as a penny. Some have grown faster and larger than others. These are called "picklers," and may be found in all grocery stores, bottled for table use. Picklers are worth $1.60 to $2.50 a bushel, and generally about 600 bushels are gathered to an acre. After these primes or picklers have been sorted out, the culls or very small onions (sets) are placed in large trays and remain there until perfectly dry; then they are kept till spring, at which time they are set out in fields. Men are employed to keep all weeds away from them and to keep the ground constantly loosened up all around. Level, shallow cultivation is best. The sets that were planted first as seeds more than a year ago, have by July 4th developed into good-sized onions; and men go down the rows with diggers which throw the onions out, and then they are piled up and are ready for the "toppers." The toppers cut the roots and stalks off and place the onions in baskets and sacks, ready for the market. All of the onions are not dug, however; the grower allows an acre or two to keep on growing till the stalks are four or five feet high. On the very top large seed-balls grow, and when ripe they are cut from the onion—which some growers allow to remain in the ground until the next year, thus getting a double crop of seed from each onion. Good ground will yield about 400 pounds of seed to an acre and 300 or more bushels of big onions for market.

Marketing.—In regard to "bunch" or early green onions, an Illinois grower writes: Don't begin on the onions till they are large enough so that not more than five or six are required to make a bunch.

See to it that the bunches are uniform in size, and that the onions are clean and bright (see picture). It is very hard to forecast the onion market. Some seasons the early market is the best; at other times the best prices are obtained later. Styles of shipping crates vary in different localities. Here we use a flat crate

"BUNCHING." HAVE BUNCHES UNIFORM IN SIZE AND ONIONS CLEAN

holding ten dozen bunches; it has a division through the center. The onions, after they are bunched and tied, are cut in lengths about an inch shorter than the space between the ends of the crate and the division board. In packing, the bunches are placed lengthwise of the crate. By placing the butts of the first layer snugly against the end of the crate, and those of the next against the division board, an inch space is left between each layer of onions. This space affords ventilation and prevents heating.

DIGGING ONIONS WITH A HAND HARVESTER

M a t u r e d bulbs or large onions are left in the field until most of the necks (don't wait for all) wither, turn yellow, and the tops fall over; then they are pulled by hand or dug out (see picture) with a U-shaped "onion-harvester" attachment which is made for wheel hoes, thrown into small windrows (three or four rows in one), and allowed to dry and cure for several days (if the weather is wet, the curing may have to be done in shed or barn). Then, with shears or knife, the tops are cut off about half an inch above each bulb (see illustration); cutting too close rots the onion, too long looks untidy. They may now be gathered up, graded into different sizes, packed in ventilated baskets, barrels, crates, etc. (as your market demands), and sold at once. Or they may be stored (according to directions on page 80).

"TOPPING." THE TOPS ARE CUT OFF ABOUT HALF AN INCH ABOVE EACH ONION

BULBLETS

"Scullions" or "scallions" are onions which grow a thick neck and fail to bottom out. Inferior seed or too wet a soil may cause the trouble.

If the onion tops are still green in early September, roll a barrel along the rows and break them down. This helps to check growth and hastens the withering process.

One-half ounce of onion seed is required for about 100 feet of drill. About four pounds per acre. Sets, one quart to perhaps forty feet of row; about eight bushels or more to the acre.

There are three kinds of onion sets: 1, onions grown from any common variety of seed, and not allowed to mature—thus producing little white, red or yellow "sets," according to the kind of seed sown; 2, sets that are produced in a cluster above ground on the stalk end of a peculiar variety called "Egyptian," "top" or "tree" onion; and, 3, "multiplier" or "potato onion" sets which are produced in a cluster underground in the odd way common to this distinct variety. Each kind of set, if planted, of course keeps and reproduces its own characteristics.

Winter storage of onions requires experience, and even then is usually attended with more or less loss; but the practise often pays. Onions may be wintered, says Farmers' Bulletin No. 39, by two different processes, namely, by freezing the bulbs and keeping them in this state all winter, or by storing them in shallow bins in a *dry* apartment (not in a cellar) where the temperature can be maintained just above the freezing point. The freezing process is satisfactory only in the extreme North, where the weather is cold during the entire winter. It consists in simply storing the bulbs in the barn or outbuilding, allowing them to freeze, then covering with hay, straw, or bags, and letting cover remain on the bulbs until they gradually thaw out with the rising temperature of the spring. A layer of hay must be thrown on the floor or bottom of the bins before putting in the onions. The temperature of the bins should not run above 32° or below 15° until spring. *Too severe freezing or successive freezing and thawing will injure the bulbs.* Onions not thoroughly dry when stored will sprout and spoil.

Insects and diseases: The principal enemies of the onion are the onion maggot, a tiny white worm which burrows in the bulb; and onion smut or rot, a blackish fungous disease. For the first the most effective remedy is a change of location of the onion field each year. This may be followed by any of the treatments recommended by John B. Smith in his

Economic Entomology: "Keep a close watch for the first signs of maggots, and lift out and destroy infested plants that have wilted down. Turn away the earth from the rows with a hand plow so as to expose the root system in part, then broadcast about 600 pounds of kainit and 100 pounds nitrate of soda per acre; turn back the earth to the plants. The application is best made just before or during, or immediately after, a rain * * * Bisulphide of carbon injected below the root system has been used with success." (On small areas only, I presume. An injector or large syringe or a machine-oil can may be used for the purpose.—J. B.) "It should be used when the soil is moist but not water-soaked * * * Tobacco dust, soot, wood ashes, etc., applied early around the base of the plants * * * Carbolic acid emulsion poured about the base of infested plants." (See Chapter V for formula.) Fall-plowing is a help, too—particularly if you will scatter a little grain on the field occasionally afterwards and then turn on a flock of chickens. Smut is held in check to some extent by rotation of crops, by transplanting, and by gathering and burning infected specimens and refuse. A mixture of equal parts of sulphur and lime sown in the drills with the seed has given good results as a remedy for the disease. Or the seed might be treated with formalin as advised for cabbage in Chapter XI. Cutworms are sometimes troublesome in the onion field (see Chapter XI for remedies). Thrips (tiny, yellow insects that suck the juices from the leaves) may be killed by spraying with whale-oil soap solution or kerosene emulsion. Downy mildew sometimes affects onion tops on low ground. Remedies: Destroy diseased onions and spray plants early in the season with the Bordeaux mixture—which spray would also be a help to keep smut in check.

AN INSECT DESTROYER

TWELVE-ACRE POTATO FIELD, FREEHOLD, N. J. AVERAGED 473 BUSHELS TO THE ACRE—A FINE CROP

Chapter VIII

PEAS AND POTATOES

"A garden is the personal part of an estate—that area which is most intimately associated with the private life of the home."

P EAS, like onions, are hardy, and early varieties should be sown in the open ground just as soon as soil conditions will permit—in March or early April in the North, and in December, January or February farther south (according to latitude).

A *too* rich soil is not good for this crop, I have discovered, for an excess of nitrogen is likely to cause the plants to "run all to vines." A light clay loam is desirable if extra early peas are wanted. Peas are nitrogenous—that is, they have the power of gathering nitrogen from the air.

Rows in the small garden may be about three feet apart for single rows of tall-growing varieties, that are to be supplied with some support for the vines to climb upon. (Rows of dwarf varieties might be narrower.) A method often practised, however, is to plant double rows (about eight inches apart) with aisles about three feet wide (six inches wider would be better for horse cultivation) between each two double-rows. The vine support for this double row is placed in the center of the eight-inch space, so that vines in both rows may climb on the one support (and thus form a single trellis of vines from a double row of plants).

Early plantings of peas are usually covered about three inches deep; later sowings, when the ground is drier, are often covered four or five inches deep in mellow, light soil. Personally, I favor deep planting for all peas in the well-drained garden—five or six inches if soil conditions will permit. If this is practised, it is safer to cover the seed only about three inches at first, putting the remainder of the covering into the furrow when the pea sprouts are just coming through the first covering. This double-covering precaution insures the ability of the sprouts to push through to the surface, and is especially necessary in heavy soils. One quart will sow about 100 feet of

HAND-SOWING OF PEAS IN FURROWS. ('TIS BETTER TO SOW LARGE AREAS WITH A SEED DRILL)

single drill; about one and a half bushels to an acre. Thinning is seldom necessary. Open the furrows with a hoe or a plow or a culti-vator rigged as a fur-rower, and drop the seed by hand in a continuous row. (Ex-tensive growers, of course, plant with a seed drill.) Use plenty of seed, for rot, cutworms, etc., may get part of it.

Keep down weeds. When the plants are two or three inches above ground, furnish some support for them to climb on—"brush," sticks, wire-netting, wires, cord, or whatever is handy. Continue to cultivate until the crop is gathered, then pull out and remove the vines and trellis, loosen up the ground, and plant to some other crop. (NOTE: Peas require a cool season and do not do well in the hot weather of mid-summer; so they are an early-season crop that permits of a following crop of something else—late cabbage, celery, etc. Successional sowings of peas should be made every ten days until June, thus securing a regular succession of bearing vines. In the North, dwarf varieties of peas are sometimes sown in early August for a fall crop.)

Field culture: Let me say that the gardener who grows peas on a large scale for market or canning factory, as a rule plants and handles his crop somewhat differently from the smaller grower. For one thing, he generally sows the seed with a hand or horse planter, thus combining in one operation the opening, seeding and covering of the furrows. And because he uses a machine which does the covering all in one dose, he is apt to plant the seed more shallow—so as to make sure that the pea shoots will, without double-covering, be able to push through the soil. He usually plants early peas about two inches deep; and, later, when the soil is drier, he plants about three inches deep.

For another thing, he generally s p a c e s the single rows f a r t h e r apart (about five feet for the very tall-growing varieties, less for the dwarf kinds), so that the vines may

AN INEXPENSIVE CORD SUPPORT FOR PEAS. WIRE POULTRY-NETTING IS BETTER

have room to sprawl on the ground and thus save the great bother and expense of furnishing extensive areas with something for the vines to climb on. Two or three cultivations with horse implements are given, and then the vines are allowed to grow as they please. After the vines have attained size and have fallen over, they need turning every two or three days or they may rot on the under side; simply "flop" them gently over from one side to the other, using a long, round stick for the purpose.

Picking and marketing: Peas are at their best when the pods have filled out plump but have not become hard. For large areas, pickers will need to be hired; they should be instructed not to tear the vines, to pick only marketable pods, and not to leave on them long pieces of vine. Each variety should be kept by itself, and no over-ripe yellow-looking pods should be packed. Peas are sold in a variety of packages—in bags, ventilated barrels, baskets, crates, etc. For long-distance shipment the small package is preferable, for peas in bulk are likely to heat and spoil in a short time. A round, one-third-barrel veneer basket is a favorite Maryland and New Jersey package for peas. In some localities near canning factories, peas can be profitably grown under contract for the factories.

Varieties: There are two types of seed—the smooth and the wrinkled. There are short and tall varieties of both types. My experience is that wrinkled kinds are superior in quality, but if planted very early are more likely to rot in the ground than the smooth varieties. Among the extra-early kinds, the following are well-known: First of All, Nott's Excelsior, American Wonder, Daniel O'Rourke, Little Gem. Mid-season: Shropshire Hero, Abundance, Advancer, Heroine. Late: Telephone, Stratagem, Champion of England, Yorkshire Hero, Marrowfat.

Insects and diseases: Often the tips of the vines are covered with little green aphis (lice). Any of the sprays for lice mentioned in Chapter V will kill them. The following two methods, however, have been used with better success: 1. On a very hot day the lice may be brushed from the vines into the paths and covered with the cultivator, says S. A. Johnson. This method does not work well where the ground is lumpy, for the lice crawl out and back upon the plants, unless the dirt is sufficiently firm to smother them. 2. They may be brushed into pans which are dragged between the rows. To do this, have galvanized iron pans made about six feet long, eighteen inches wide and six inches deep. Put a thin layer of kerosene in the bottom. Drag the pan between the rows while two boys brush the vines toward the pan. There should be sufficient oil in the pan to insure the wetting of all the lice, and it should be cleaned and the oil renewed whenever necessary. (A. D. Taylor, Massachusetts, writes that he has had best success by dusting the vines when wet with dew with dry hardwood ashes.)

Weevils are more or less troublesome to both peas and beans. 'Tis said that late plantings are not so likely to be infested by weevils. This insect eats out the heart of the seed, and is hatched from eggs that are laid on the green pod while it is growing on the vine. There is no means known to prevent the laying of the eggs or the entrance of the larvæ into the seed. The only direct means of fighting the pest is to kill the larvæ in the dry seed before planting, preferably with bisulphide of carbon. Put seed in a close box, throw a cloth over the seed, pour the liquid over this cloth, and put on the lid. Leave undisturbed for forty-eight hours. Be careful not to inhale the vapor or bring a lighted lamp near it, as it is poisonous and explosive. Use about one ounce to four bushels of seed. Another method is to put the seed in water; infested seed will float on the surface and may be skimmed off and burned.

Cutworms: See Chapter XI.

Mildew and rust occasionally attack this crop, particularly if the weather is unusually damp. If your vines begin to wilt and turn yellow, fungous disease of the stem near the ground is probably to blame. Spraying with the Bordeaux mixture is a preventive of these troubles if done early enough.

POTATOES.—The ground should be rich. Many growers secure excellent results by annually broadcasting about 1,000 pounds per acre of a complete fertilizer containing plenty of potash. Stable manure is good to loosen up clay soils, but where the potato scab is prevalent, the constant use of large quantities of stable manure is believed to increase this fungous trouble. Potatoes do best in a loose, well-drained loam, well provided with humus. A clover sod or a crop of cowpeas, etc., plowed under in the fall, makes an ideal field for me. Owing to scab and other potato peculiarities, the potato grower needs to practise a systematic rotation of crops.

Medium-sized seed is best. To start with, buy northern-grown seed; then each year at digging time, select tubers for seed from the best hills. Avoid "Jumboes" or "littles." Treat the seed with formalin (see Chapter V) to prevent scab. Cellar-sprouted tubers are not so good for seed as those which are unsprouted. Tubers sprouted a little in sunlight just previous to planting are desirable when extra early crops are wanted. Just how to cut the seed is a disputed point, but those who cut so as to leave at least two strong eyes on each seed piece, will make no mistake. Some people discard the "seed-end" of each tuber. It requires ten or more bushels of potatoes to seed one acre.

An important point is to have the soil in perfect condition before planting. Use the harrow thoroughly. Rows, for horse cultivation, should be about three feet apart. Drop seed pieces about fifteen inches apart; cover about four inches deep; shallower planting would bring the crop too near the surface and cause portions of the tubers to sunburn and turn green. The two illustrations show the results of wrong and right planting depths. There are several good machine potato-planters now on the market; but on small areas it is customary to open the furrows with a plow or horse cultivator or hand hoe and drop the seed by hand, and then cover the seed in a similar manner.

TOO-SHALLOW PLANT-ING, RESULTING IN SUNBURNED POTA-TOES TOO NEAR THE SURFACE

Cultivation should begin soon after the seed is planted. Go diagonally over the field with a light

PLANTED RIGHT—
FOUR INCHES DEEP.
RESULT : NO SUN-
BURNED TUBERS

spike-tooth harrow, to break up the soil crust and to kill any weeds which may start. Go over the field again within a week, the other way d i a g o n a l l y. These early harrowings greatly lessen the after work of keeping the field clean. When the potatoes are several inches high, a cultivator should be used between rows. If the ground is well-drained and if the seed is planted sufficiently deep, hilling-up is unnecessary. One hand hoeing during the season may be desirable.

Insects and diseases: Every few weeks I spray the vines with a mixture of the full-strength Bordeaux and Paris green. Spraying should begin when the plants are about four inches high and continue as long as growth lasts. Thus bugs, early and late blight, mildew, rot, etc., may usually be kept in check with one combined mixture. The potato-stalk weevil which sometimes bores in the stalks, can be kept down by prompt gathering and burning of vines when the crop is dug; badly infested vines should be pulled and burned at any time.

Wireworms (not angleworms) are very slender, yellowish, hard-bodied worms that are often troublesome in the soil; usually, however, these pests dislike ground which has been heavily enriched with chemical fertilizers; 'tis said that fall-plowing, followed by a spring application of 150 pounds of nitrate of soda, and 1,000 pounds of kainit to the acre, is particularly good to conquer wireworms. This should be sown broadcast and harrowed in before the crop is planted. (This is for the worms, mainly, and is not a balanced fertilizer mixture. Some bone meal or phosphate might be added to help balance the food needs of the plant). Repeat the practise

HAND-PLANTING OF POTATOES; OPENING AND CLOSING THE FURROWS WITH A PLOW

for several years, and turn the hens on the field whenever possible—particularly after plowing or harrowing.

Varieties: Each locality has its favorites; study

your market's requirements. Among the best early varieties I might mention: Early Rose, Early Michigan, Early Ohio, Early Norther, Early Bovee, Early White Ohio, etc. Among the best late or main-crop varieties, are: Rural New-Yorker, Carman No. 3, Sir Walter Raleigh, Great Divide, Vermont Gold Coin, Nebraska, Mammoth Pearl, Rose Seedling, Burbank, Uncle Sam, State of Maine, etc.

In the North early potatoes, like peas, are planted in March or April as soon as the ground becomes dry enough (tubers will rot if planted in too wet a soil). Fall plowing is, of course, a help to early planting; so is tile draining. The plant is sensitive to frost, but usually the sprouts take so long a time to get above ground that frost danger is mostly over before they appear; at a critical time,

A MACHINE POTATO-PLANTER OPENS THE FURROWS, PLANTS THE SEED, COVERS IT AND MARKS THE NEXT ROW

however, 'tis possible, I find, to plow or hoe a little soil on to the tender sprouts and thus outwit Jack Frost. Main or late crop potatoes are planted in the North any time between about May 10th and June 1st. In Georgia early potatoes are planted about February 1st, I am told.

"Second-crop potatoes": In some of the southern states a double cropping system is practised, the second crop being grown the same season from seed produced by the first crop. For full particulars about this method, write to the United States Department of Agriculture, Washington, D. C., and ask for free Farmers' Bulletin No. 35.

Digging, storing and marketing: The maturity and death of the vines show that it is time to dig the main or late crop, which should be done at once if the tubers seem to be rotting; but if they are keeping all right it may be better to delay digging until later in the fall when the weather is cooler. Early-market tubers are dug whenever big enough, regardless of the vines. In the fall choose a dry time to do the digging, if possible. They should be dug by hand if the area is not large—using a four-tined potato hook made for the purpose. Or, if the area is large, there are excellent horse-power machine diggers and pickers that save much time and labor.

In harvesting, as well as in storage, potatoes should be exposed to light as little as possible. After digging I advise that they should lie on the ground only long enough to dry thoroughly, and then be gathered up into slatted bushel-crates, piled on the wagon, hauled to the packing or storage place and sorted into grades (a machine potato-sorter is made that facilitates this work). In some cases the potatoes are sorted in the field and packed at once in barrels, or in burlap sacks holding 110 to 120 pounds. Early potatoes are sold in Maryland and some other states in round one-third-barrel veneer baskets. Late potatoes are often shipped in barrels with the tops tied with burlap, or in burlap sacks, or loose in carload lots.

In storing potatoes a dark, dry place and a low temperature is required. The potato tuber is uninjured by a temperature of 33° F. Warmth, light and moisture favor sprouting, which injures potatoes both for planting and eating. Storage in cellars is very common; outdoor pits are sometimes used (consult Chapter IX in regard to pits). No matter how stored, the winter loss from shrinkage, rot, etc., must always be considered. It is often wiser to sell in the fall if a fair price is offered. If stored in a dugout or cellar, put the potatoes in bins made of slats (to insure ventilation) and not more than five feet deep.

Indoor cellars: Generally speaking I would earnestly say that a *house* cellar is not a good place to store large quantities of vegetables—not good for the folks above, and not good for the vegetables because usually too warm. However, it is often advisable to have small lots of potatoes, roots, etc., in the cellar. Put the potatoes in bins. Roots should be packed in or covered with sand to keep them from drying out and shriveling. Ventilate the cellar, and promptly remove any vegetable which has rotted. Keep out light, frost and warmth.

AFTER RADISHES ARE PULLED, SOME MARKET GARDENERS SOAK THEM
IN WATER FOR THREE HOURS TO MAKE THEM EXTRA CRISP

CHAPTER IX

ROOT CROPS

BEET, CARROT, PARSNIP, RADISH, SALSIFY,
TURNIP, ETC.

THE long-rooted varieties require a *deep, loose* soil for their best development (the round or stump-rooted kinds will, of course, do well in shallower soil). Subsoiling or tile draining are great aids in growing long-rooted crops. Plenty of fertilizer and humus is necessary. These crops are all hardy and therefore permit of early sowing. Give thorough cultivation and hand weeding. Transplanting is seldom practised with these vegetables.

BEET.—There are two kinds—the early-season, quick-growing, round, short-rooted varieties, and the long-rooted, long-season ones. The former are most often grown of late years for market, and may be sown in early spring as an early crop to be followed by something else, or in July or early August as a succession crop after some earlier crop has matured. (The long-rooted kinds are generally sown in May or June in the North, and grow during the entire season.)

Sow in drills about a foot apart for wheel-hoe cultivation; two and a half feet for horse work. Thin the plants gradually to about five inches apart. Cover seed about an inch deep. The seed germinates slowly and a preliminary soaking hastens germination. One ounce of seed will sow about fifty feet of drill; about five pounds to the acre.

Beet "greens" are popular, and are merely young plants that are only partly grown. They are usually obtained in the form of "thinnings" from the rows, leaving the remaining plants to mature. Beet greens are sold in bunches, leaves and all.

Early beets are marketed in various ways—generally tied in bunches of six with part or all of the top attached. Main-crop beets are topped and packed in barrels, etc.

Varieties: Among early kinds, these are my favorites: Early Egyptian, Eclipse, Crimson Globe. Long Blood is a standard late variety.

Insects and diseases: These, as a rule, are seldom troublesome. Wireworms in the soil sometimes

THE HAND-THINNING OF ROOT CROPS IS AN EARLY AND IMPORTANT DETAIL

hurt the roots (see Chapter VIII for remedies). Root rot is occasionally serious; lime applied to the soil is a help. Beet rust and leaf-spot are fungous troubles on the leaves; remedy, Bordeaux spray applied early. Rotation of crops is useful in all these troubles.

CARROT.—For early use, plant the Short Horn, Oxheart and similar short-rooted varieties early in the spring. Main-crop carrots for winter use (Danver's Half-long, Long Orange, etc.,) may be sown in the North in early June, following early radishes, etc.

The seed germinates slowly (soaking helps) and the young plants are easily ruined by weeds or neglect; but when once established the crop is an easy one. Sow the seed thickly, about half an inch deep; rows and thinning the same as for beets. One ounce of seed will sow about 100 feet of drill; about two and a half pounds required for an acre. Americans eat very few carrots and the market demand is therefore rather limited and uncertain. Fungi or insects are not usually troublesome.

PARSNIP.—This is an all-season crop and should be sown as early in the spring as the soil can be worked. Sown and thinned the same as carrots, except that one ounce of seed will sow about 200 feet of drill; five pounds about one acre. The seed germinates slowly. Varieties: For shallow soils plant Early Round French, but if your soil is deep enough plant Hollow Crown, Guernsey or Half-long. For table use, parsnips are sweeter and better if they are allowed to stay in the ground and freeze— digging them in late winter or when thaws occur; for immediate use a portion of the crop might be dug and stored in the fall. There are practically no troublesome insects or diseases. Marketable roots should be long, straight and smooth, and not branched (shallow or lumpy soil causes branching, says Farmer Vincent).

RADISH.—For best results I choose a sandy loam, well drained and enriched. This crop, to be eatable or marketable, must be grown quickly—pushed along from start to finish so as to be crisp and juicy. Begin to sow the seed outdoors in the North in March or April (earlier farther south) as soon as the ground can be worked. For wheel-hoe cultivation the rows should be about a foot apart. Sow the seed rather thinly, cover about one-half inch deep, and thin the plants to about three inches apart. The seed germinates very quickly and the crop is ready in five or six weeks, usually. Successional sowings may be made at ten-day intervals until June, so as to have radishes in good condition all through the radish season. In July and August this crop does not do so well, and is seldom planted then. One ounce of seed should sow about 100 feet of drill; ten pounds about one acre. Radishes are occasionally grown in hotbeds or coldframes for very early market.

AFTER SOAKING, RADISHES ARE PLACED ON A WIRE-NETTING RINSING TRAY, ROOTS ALL ONE WAY

Winter radishes are not much in favor in this country, but those who like them may sow the seed about September 1st, and expect a crop before freezing weather.

Marketing: After radishes are pulled, some market gardeners soak them for three hours in barrels of water, to make them extra crisp (see full-page picture facing this chapter). Next they are placed on a wire-netting rinsing tray, roots all one way; third, they are rinsed with a stream of fresh water (see two illustrations in this chapter). Then they are tied in bunches, leaves left on, and are ready to sell or to pack for shipment. Different shipping packages are used in different localities.

Varieties: Among the best-known early short-rooted kinds are Scarlet Globe, Round Red, White Turnip, French Breakfast, Half-long Deep Scarlet, etc. Early long-rooted: Early Scarlet Short Top. White Chinese is a good winter variety.

Insects: Usually the only serious pest is a maggot in the soil. This is similar to the onion maggot mentioned in Chapter VII, and the remedies would be the same as there given. Flea beetles sometimes bother (see Chapter XI).

SALSIFY.—This is also called "vegetable oyster," and is often used by Harriet in making an imitation oyster-stew. It is grown the same as parsnip; it is hardy and may be left in the ground over winter or stored at once. One ounce of seed will sow about 100 feet of drill. Mammoth Sandwich

AFTER A THOROUGH RINSING, RADISHES ARE THEN READY TO BE TIED IN BUNCHES

Island is a good variety. There are no troublesome pests so far as I know.

TURNIP.—Usually sown as a fall crop in July or early August; sometimes sown as an early market crop very early in the spring. Must be grown rapidly or the roots are woody and bitter. Sow in the spring in rows the same as radishes. The maggot, wireworm and flea beetle are the principal pests (see elsewhere for remedies). Thin the plants to about five inches apart for early; wider if you want big roots.

Instead of sowing in rows in July, it is quite a common practise to broadcast the seed on clean, mellow ground, and then harrow or rake it in. Here's a better way: Have the seedbed very fine, then roll it; sow the seed soon *after* a rain, and cover by lightly rolling the ground. Of course no subsequent cultivation is given. The yield is often very good when seed is sown in this way, but row culture is usually more certain and satisfactory. One ounce of seed will sow about 200 feet of drill. Use about two pounds to the acre, either broadcast or in rows. For horse cultivation space the rows two feet and a half apart. Early turnips are sometimes bunched like beets, or they may be topped and sold in barrels, baskets, etc. Consult your market's requirements. The late crop should be gathered *before* hard freezing begins, topped and sold or stored.

Varieties: Purple-top Strap-leaf, Early Milan, Flat Dutch, Early Munich, Purple-top White Globe, etc.

SOME OTHER ROOT CROPS.—Sugar beets are grown in some localities, under contract, for beet-sugar factories, and the varieties used are known to be especially rich in sugar contents; they are grown the same as other beets, but are sold by the ton. Mangel-wurzel is a mammoth species of coarse beet which grows partially above ground and is well liked as a stock food. Rutabaga, or Swedish turnip, is usually grown as a food for stock. None of the three foregoing varieties are, strictly speaking, garden vegetables.

DIGGING AND STORING ROOT CROPS.—Roots may be dug out or pulled out; but if the crop is large or the roots long, I find that it is easier to plow them out. For storing or shipping in the fall, the roots should dry in the sun until the soil will shake from them, and the tops should be cut off, about an inch above the crown. Then haul to pit, cellar or packing house. Be careful not to bruise when digging or handling; bruised or mutilated roots will not keep long.

Storing: The construction of a Colorado-style storage house or dugout is simple, says E. R. Bennett. An excavation is made in the ground, of the required dimensions for the cellar and of a sufficient depth to give soil for covering the top. A frame of posts, timbers and rafters is then made as for a building. This frame is covered with wire-netting or brush. Over this two or three feet of straw is placed and this is covered with soil to a depth of six to twelve inches. Ventilator shafts are put in at regular intervals to give air circulation and keep the temperature from rising too high. Some of these dugouts have an alley through the center with doors at either end so that the wagon may be driven through. Double doors with a dead air space between are used as a protection against frost. If roots or potatoes are stored while the weather is yet warm, the ventilators and doors are left open *nights* to give a circulation of cold air, and *closed during the heat of the day.* In this way the bins are gradually cooled down, and by giving close attention to the temperature the whole mass is kept as cool as possible without danger from frost. During the winter considerable care has to be exercised to prevent the temperature of the dugout from rising from the heat developed by the stored roots or potatoes. This is regulated by opening and closing the ventilator shafts as the case demands. (In a wet climate it would be necessary to have some kind of water-proof roof on top of the soil, to keep out rain, etc.—J. B.)

Outdoor "pits": These differ from dugouts in that they are not usually sunken in the ground. They are, as a rule, made on the surface as follows: Piles of topped and unbruised roots (or potatoes) are made on a high, well-drained piece of ground. These piles may be almost any shape or size (but it is wise not to have the piles large enough to heat when covered—better make several separate pits when the quantity to be stored is large, or one long pit divided

AN OUTDOOR ROOT-PIT

at four-foot intervals with a wall of earth so as to make separate compartments). The accompanying picture shows how to make a pit. On top of the ground comes a shallow layer of straw, then a cone of roots not wider than about six feet at the base, then a layer of straw about six inches deep when matted down, and, lastly, a layer of soil about a foot in depth shoveled up from around the pit. In the center of each pit or compartment, is an upright stick to which is tied a wisp of straw arranged as a ventilator. (In *very* severe climates it may be necessary to put a layer of manure on top of the soil layer, or another layer each of straw and soil.) Special remarks: Do *not* cover the pit all at once. First put on the straw, with a board or two to hold it in place; this will protect against light frosts. As the weather gets colder, throw on an inch or two of soil—adding soil as the winter advances until the pit is fully protected. A house cellar is not a suitable place to store more than a few potatoes (in bins) and a few roots (in sand).

CHAPTER X

LETTUCE. CELERY.

Good "luck" with these crops means rich, moist soil, good seed, and plenty of elbow grease.—Tim.

 ETTUCE is hardy, and therefore the first sowing outdoors may be made just as early in the spring as the ground can be worked. Successional sowings may thereafter be made every two weeks, to insure a constant supply for the table or market. I like the rows about fifteen inches apart for wheel-hoe cultivation; about two and a half feet apart for horse work. Sow in drills and cover about half an inch deep. Thin the plants gradually, using the thinnings for table use as far as possible, until the plants stand about ten inches apart (more or less, according to the variety grown and the size of head wanted). The best soil for early lettuce is a light, loose loam, made very rich. Applications of nitrate of soda or liquid manure are helpful to the growing crop (see Chapter IV). One-quarter ounce of seed will sow about 100 feet of drill.

The foregoing is the easy small-garden method of growing lettuce without transplanting. Northern market gardeners, however, usually prefer to raise early plants in hotbeds, transplant to cold-frames, and then transplant to the field. Or sometimes they sow the seed outdoors in September, transplant in October to coldframes for wintering (spacing the plants about five inches apart), and then,

in the early spring, transplant the wintered lettuce
from coldframes to field; or sometimes outdoor
August-sown plants are moved to frames and forced
along for Thanksgiving or early winter market. Or,
for the later crops of head lettuce, they may sow the
seed in drills outdoors in early spring, and then, instead of thinning the lettuce, transplant it to a nicely-
prepared field where it can be set the required distance apart. Market gardeners have a custom, also,
of transplanting a head of lettuce between each two
early cabbages in a field row—the lettuce is soon
off and then the cabbages can have all the space.

Hotbed lettuce, in the North, is usually started
in February and transplanted in about four weeks
(see Chapter III for cultural directions). In the
South it may be started several weeks or months
earlier, according to latitude. One ounce of seed
should furnish about 1,000 plants; they are moved
to the open ground in March or early April. The
faster the growth, the more crisp, tender and sweet
the lettuce will be. Some gardeners facilitate the
"heading" process by drawing up the outer leaves
around the plant and securing them in place with a
string. (NOTE: Very early lettuce is often grown
entirely in frames or greenhouses, without transplanting outdoors.)

Summer and fall lettuce: Most varieties of lettuce do not do well in hot weather; therefore if you
want summer lettuce you should select the kind
called Cos—a distinct type (also known as "celery
lettuce," or Romaine). For fall lettuce any of the
spring varieties may be planted.

Varieties: Early Curled Simpson, Black Seeded
Simpson, Grand Rapids, etc., are good extra-early
kinds of the curled or leaf variety. Tennis Ball,

Boston Market, Iceberg, Hanson, etc., are good head or "cabbage" kinds, but do not mature quite so quickly.

Marketing lettuce: My experience tells me that lettuce with a blanched heart sells best in most markets, and is in more or less demand all the year around. Lettuce in the field is cut off close to the ground and taken to the packing house, where the untidy outer leaves are taken off. A favorite package for lettuce in Maryland, etc., is the round, veneer basket with a cover (the cover is not shown in illustration). Ventilated barrels, crates, etc., are used in some localities. Lettuce for shipment should be quite dry when packed. Lettuce for a near-by fancy trade is sometimes grown in two-inch pots,

A BASKET OF MARYLAND HEAD LETTUCE NEATLY PACKED

and marketed in that way—thus insuring freshness.

Insects and diseases: Out-of-doors the lettuce crop is seldom troubled by bugs or fungi. Cutworms sometimes bother (see Chapter XI). Under glass "damping off" (sometimes called "drop" or "wilt") is a common trouble (see Chapter II). Stem and leaf rot may usually be prevented, where prevalent, by covering the greenhouse or hotbed soil with two inches of sand which has been sterilized by being treated with boiling water. Half-strength Bordeaux mixture might be sprayed on the plants when they are little, as a preventive.

CELERY.—For ordinary home use celery can be grown on almost any kind of rich garden soil, but for the best market success deep alluvial or reclaimed swamp ground is the kind to choose. At

Kalamazoo, Mich., famous for its celery, the soil I saw in the fields is black, moist, and filled with humus; it lies very low and is drained by a network of open ditches.

For the early crop in the North, sow seed in hotbeds about March 1st (earlier in the South), and transplant to coldframes about April 10th (see Chapter III for cultural details). The seed germinates very slowly and the young plants are weak; plant seed rather thickly and see that the soil does not dry out until plants are well up. The plants may be moved to the open ground in May or early June. There is not a large demand for very early celery.

For the late crop, seed may be sown outdoors as early in the spring as the ground can be worked. The soil should be fine and moist. Sow in drills about a foot apart and cover about three-eighths of an inch deep, afterward firming the soil by rolling, by pressing with the feet, or by tamping with the back of a hoe-blade. If the weather is very dry, germination may be hastened by watering the seed-bed and then covering the rows with burlap until the plants are up. Start the hoe as soon as the rows can be seen. In early July dig the plants, shear or cut off a portion of the tops (read Chapter III), and transplant to rows for horse cultivation about three feet apart for the dwarf varieties or four feet for the tall kinds, plants spaced about six inches apart in the row. Be sure to firm the earth about the roots. (For small-garden culture, or where boards are used for blanching the crop, the rows may be closer together—say two or two and one-half feet apart. In fact, in a system called the "new celery culture," it is advocated that plants should be set *very* close together—about 6 x 8 inches apart—so that the leaves will meet and the plants blanch themselves; this method, however, usually requires irrigation to make it a success; the "self-blanching" varieties are used, and the outer sides of the patch are covered with boards.)

Blanching: Early or summer celery is usually blanched, after the first "handling," by standing twelve-inch-wide boards close against each side of the celery plants, the top edges hooked or cleated so as to be about three inches apart. The boards should be about twelve feet long, and are put on when the celery is about a foot high. I think that the board method is better than earth for summer blanching, because celery covered entirely with earth is more liable to rot or rust in warm weather. This blanching process requires two or three weeks after the boards are put on. Then the plants can be dug, as wanted, and sold or used. (NOTE: In very small gardens celery may easily be blanched by slipping a piece of tile over each plant.)

The late crop of celery is usually blanched by hilling earth gradually up to the plants on both sides of the row. This kind of blanching is not begun until the hot summer weather is over, the weather cool, and the plants well grown. The first part of the blanching process is called "handling." This, in plain English, means to gather together with

A HORSE-DRAWN CELERY-HILLER IS A GREAT HELP IN THE BLANCHING PROCESS

the hands a plant's sprawling leaves and stalks, bring them together in compact, upright form, and then hold them in place by drawing up and compacting enough soil around the clump of stalks. In about two weeks more earth is drawn up around the new growth. Later, a third hilling-up may be required; this, and the second one, is easily accomplished in large fields by using a horse-drawn celery-hiller sold especially for the purpose (or a one-horse plow might be used, or a cultivator rigged to throw soil toward both sides). The work must be done when the soil and celery plants are dry, as hilling or handling in a moist condition favors rust or rot, or both.

All celery requires some kind of blanching—even the so-called "self-blanching" varieties need the shade of the extra-close planting I mentioned a few paragraphs back.

Varieties: White Plume and Golden Self-Blanching are good early kinds. Kalamazoo, Golden Dwarf, Boston Market, Giant Pascal, etc., are excellent fall and winter varieties. I do not like the Giant Pascal type so well as the smaller kinds.

Packing and marketing: Celery when fully grown and blanched, is dug, and prepared for market by trimming off the roots so as to leave the short solid stem. The tops are never cut, but any loose or untidy outside stems and leaves may be removed. The stalks when thus dressed, and washed, are made into bundles of one dozen each, says W. N. Hutt, Maryland, and tied twice with light tape to hold the stalks together in position. These bundles are packed into a ventilated crate, which in Maryland is 22 x 24 inches and twenty inches high. The crate is packed full, placing the stalks in upright position. The crate will hold ten or a dozen bundles of ordinary size.

In some localities celery is shipped in crates where the bunches are laid flat and the tops lapped.

Storing: Celery will withstand considerable light frost, but its keeping qualities and flavor will be injured by hard freezing.

Large northern growers handle the last of the crop by the method known as trenching. The celery is first partially banked with earth and allowed to remain where grown so long as there is no danger from heavy frosts. Then comes the work of digging the plants to be trenched. Trenching will be greatly facilitated by setting up two parallel lines of twelve - inch boards, about eighteen or

GATHERING BOARD-BLANCHED CELERY NEAR SANFORD, FLA.—1,200 CRATES TO THE ACRE

twenty inches apart, between which the dug celery is packed with the roots embedded in the soil. When the space between the boards is filled, soil is thrown up on the outside to the tops of the boards. The boards are then lifted out and used again, the soil being allowed to come in direct contact with the celery. These trenches are usually made only fifty or sixty feet in length and are small enough to permit the removal of a whole trench at one time. As colder weather approaches, the celery is either removed and marketed or a covering of boards, straw or corn fodder is placed over the tops for protection.

Small quantities of celery, for table use, can be removed from these trenches from time to time, and stored with the roots in earth in the coolest part of the house cellar.

Insects and diseases: Insects seldom trouble the celery crop much, although sometimes celery caterpillars (pale green, with black and white marks) are bothersome. Buhach will kill them; some growers pick them off by hand. Blight, leaf spot, and rust often occur, but may be largely prevented by spraying half-strength Bordeaux mixture on the plants in the seedbed; the spray may be repeated at intervals if necessary when the plants are transplanted to the field. Rot has already been mentioned (see Blanching). Pithy stalks generally result from too much heat and not enough moisture when the young plants are growing in the field; inferior seed is also often the cause.

CHAPTER XI

CABBAGE AND CAULIFLOWER

ALSO BROCCOLI, BRUSSELS SPROUTS, KALE, KOHLRABI

EARLY cabbage should be started in hot-beds about February 1st in the North (earlier in the South), and transplanted to coldframes in about a month. Do not force cabbage along too rapidly; aim to have short, stocky plants rather than tall, spindling ones. (See Chapter III for cultural directions.) If well hardened off, the plants can usually be transplanted to the open ground early in April. A heavily-fertilized sandy or clay loam, well drained and fine and mellow, is good. Applications of nitrate of soda or liquid manure are a help in hurrying the plants along in the field (see Chapter IV). The cabbage is a gross feeder and requires large quantities of manure, fertilizer and moisture. For hoe cultivation the rows may be about two feet apart; for horse work about two and one-half feet. Space the plants about sixteen inches apart (more or less, according to variety; Early Jersey Wakefield—the favorite very early kind—is sometimes set only fourteen inches apart in the rows, while Early Summer, Succession, All-Head, All-Seasons, etc., do better at eighteen inches). Young cabbage plants are sometimes used for greens, and are then called "collards"; the true collard, however, is a kind of kale much grown in the South.

Late cabbage plants are usually grown in a seed-bed outdoors, planting the seed in April or early May in the northern states, in rows about a foot apart. Cover seed about half an inch deep. One ounce of seed will sow about 300 feet of drill and should furnish about 2,000 plants. Transplant to the field in June or early July—as a succession crop to follow some earlier vegetable. Late cabbage may be

EARLY JERSEY WAKEFIELD IS A FAVORITE EARLY CABBAGE

planted on heavier, wetter soils than should the early crop; some of the best late cabbage fields I have ever seen were on black-looking bottom lands that would do equally well for celery. Field rows for large, late varieties should not be closer than two and one-half feet; plants about two feet apart in the row. (Extensive growers often set cabbage 2½ x 2½ feet, and cultivate with a horse *both ways*—thus saving much hand hoeing.) If cabbage heads show signs of bursting, pull the head enough to break some of the roots. This helps to stop excessive growth. Danish Ball, Late Flat Dutch, Drumhead, Surehead, etc., are well-known late varieties for June setting (if the setting is delayed until early July, the crop will be more likely to mature if you use second-early varieties such as Succession, All-Head, etc.). Red cabbage and Savoy cabbage are liked by some people.

Marketing cabbage: A considerable portion of the late cabbage crop is handled in bulk. Some growers sell by the ton to kraut factories. The best carrier for shipping early cabbage is the barrel-sized crate.

Storing late cabbage: It is a mistake to delay harvesting the winter crop until the outer leaves have been frozen hard several times and when there is danger of unbroken winter weather, says Pennsylvania Bulletin No. 147. In this state it is not safe to postpone harvesting later than the tenth of November. Various methods of storing winter cabbage are used with good success. The Danish Ball is the best keeper that can be grown. In large producing districts, frost-proof storage houses are designed and built especially for the purpose. Many growers store in barns or caves. Some pile or store the untrimmed heads in protected spots, as along fences, covering after severe weather begins with straw, corn stalks, leaves or other coarse material. Burying is a favorite plan

ONE WAY OF STORING CABBAGE —CORNSTALKS ALL AROUND

with some, and there is no better way to preserve cabbage in a fresh, crisp condition: Line up on a well-drained part of the ground three rows of heads, placed close together, turned upside down. Then with a team and plow, draw two furrows, throwing soil as much as possible on the cabbage. Then finish with shovels, placing five or six inches of soil on the heads. After the ground is frozen to the depth of an inch or two, cover with strawy manure to the depth of several inches.

Insects and diseases: Root maggots are a serious

pest; consult Chapter VII for general remedies. One of the most successful remedies (for cabbage or cauliflower) is the use of pads of tarred paper. The pads are cut in a hexagonal form in order to economize the material, and a thinner grade of tarred paper than the ordinary roofing felt is used. The dotted lines in the illustration represent slits or cuts in each piece. Pads should be about two and one-half inches in diameter; one thickness of paper is enough. By having a steel die made, the complete pads can be quickly and easily punched out. The pads should be placed about the plants at the time of transplanting to the open ground. To place one, bend it slightly, to open the slit, then slip it on the plant, the stem entering the slit, after which spread the pad out flat, and press the points formed by the star-shaped cut snugly around the stem. When in place, the pad rests flat on the ground, completely encircling the stem and fitting *tightly* around it— the idea being to prevent the root-maggot fly from depositing her eggs on stem near the ground. Plants while in the seedbed should be protected with mosquito-netting.

Cabbage worms—green and plentiful—are well known to every cabbage grower; they are the larvæ of the white butterflies which fly around cabbage fields. Remedies: The main secret of success is regular, persistent treatment nearly every week. One treatment alone does little good, owing to the fact that new egg supplies are being placed on the cabbages by the butterflies all summer. Buhach is a safe and an excellent remedy to use (see Chapter V). Hot water: Water at a temperature of 130°

will kill every worm it touches without injuring the plants. Kerosene emulsion: An excellent remedy while the plants are young, but may give the heads a bad taste if used too late. Air-slaked lime: Some growers say that this (or, in fact, fine dry road dust, or any powdery substance) will kill every worm it covers.

Cutworms work only at night. These worms like to eat through the stems of cabbages, cauliflower, tomatoes, etc. Several methods of combating cutworms have been invented, such as killing them with poisoned bait scattered along the plant rows, etc., but one of the best ways is to fence them out. Cut some stiff paper (tar-paper is good) into strips about eight inches long and two inches wide. Put a strip around a plant's stem, tightly lap the edges an inch, and push the lower half of the circle into the soil— to anchor it and to prevent worms from burrowing beneath. Have the circle an inch away from stem.

Flea beetles have in recent years been destructive to young cabbage, radish and turnip plants. Tobacco dust, applied freely, will usually drive the pests away. Lime flavored with Paris green will also help in most cases. In the seedbed the plants can be protected with mosquito-netting.

Lice often attack cabbage. Remedies are given in Chapter V.

Club-root is the most common and dangerous cabbage and cauliflower disease. There is no cure, but there are preventive measures. Infected plants, refuse in cabbage fields, etc., should be burned. Rotation of crops should be practised. Lime used liberally on cabbage ground is an excellent preventive. The disease, however, usually makes its first appearance in the seedbed, and can there be best treated. The roots become swollen and distorted, and the leaves look sickly. Treating the seedbed soil with bisulphide of carbon, before planting, has been recommended. It might also be advisable to treat the seed, before sowing, as follows: Put the seed in a cloth sack and soak for two hours in a solution of one ounce of formalin in about three and one-quarter gallons of water; dry and sow at once. Or try the onion-smut remedy (lime and sulphur) given in Chapter VII.

CAULIFLOWER.—This vegetable is grown in practically the same way as cabbage, but I find that it is a much more difficult crop to bring to perfection. It succeeds best in a cool and moist climate, and in a rich, moist soil. Irrigation is a great help. Buy only the best seed; and push growth steadily along by regular cultivation. After the head forms, tie the

IF YOU CAN'T HOE OUT EVERY WEED, BE HUMBLE AND PULL 'EM

leaves together over it to prevent sunburning. Early Snowball or Early Dwarf Erfurt may be started in hotbeds about February 1st, and transplanted in the s a m e manner as advised for early cabbage. Algiers and Veitch's A u t u m n Giant may be started in an outdoor seedbed the same as late cabbage. When prepared for market, the leaves are usually neatly trimmed off even with top of head, and the heads are packed in baskets, crates, etc. Insects and diseases are the same as those that infest cabbage; which may also be said of the following vegetables:

BROCCOLI.—Not much known in this country. Very similar to the late varieties of cauliflower.

BRUSSELS SPROUTS.—Belongs to the cabbage family, but instead of forming a large head, miniature sprouts or cabbages are borne along the stem—which sprouts are considered a delicacy when young and tender. Usually grown as a late crop, by sowing seeds outdoors in June and transplanting about August 1st. Light freezing does not hurt the crop. Or an early crop may be grown and cultivated the same as cabbage.

KALE.—This is a form of cabbage which does not head; its large leaves are used for greens, and it is sometimes called "borecole." Kale is sown outdoors in the North in the spring, and is not usually transplanted. Rows the same as for cabbage plants; thin the plants to about fifteen inches apart. Kale is very hardy and is improved by freezing.

Sea-kale: Differs from the foregoing and is little known in this country. A spring vegetable, says Long Island Agronomist, earlier than asparagus. From seed sown in May good plants can be set, like asparagus, into a permanent bed in September and will remain for years. Earth is lightly piled over the bed to a height of about a foot in early spring, and when the shoots come through this covering they are cut off to the roots. This gives stalks of kale much resembling celery; pull the leaves apart as you would celery, cook in boiling salted water until tender and serve with drawn butter, with or without vinegar, as taste desires.

KOHLRABI.—This is a turnip-rooted cabbage, and the tuber is the edible part. Not much grown in the United States. Hardy. Sow the same as kale, and use the bulbs when young and tender.

WHEN SHAPE OF LIMA BEANS IS EASILY SEEN IN THE PODS, 'TIS ABOUT TIME TO PICK THEM. EIGHT THOUSAND HILLS IN THIS FIELD

CHAPTER XII

CORN. BEANS. SWEET POTATOES.

*"Great helper in the cook's rare art,
The complete garden does its part."*

SWEET or sugar corn will do nicely on almost any warm, well-drained, fairly-rich soil; it does especially well, I can testify, on a turned-under clover sod. It is a tender plant and sowings should not be made in the North until early in May. In the garden, corn may best be planted in rows about four feet apart (not in hills like the farmers' field corn). Sow the seed thinly in drills and cover about two inches deep (see Chapter V in regard to tarring the seed), and thin the plants when well up to about eight inches apart. Cultivate, thoroughly. Make successional sowings at ten-day intervals, until about July 15th. Corn is usually sold at retail by the dozen ears, and is shipped in various kinds of packages— crates, barrels, baskets, sacks, etc. The ears are not good unless pulled at just the right stage of juicy development.

Varieties: Cory, Crosby, Early Minnesota, Black Mexican, etc., are good early and second-early kinds. Country Gentleman, Stowell's Ever-green, etc., are standard late varieties. I grow all of these.

Insects and diseases: Wireworms in the soil are often troublesome (see Chapter VIII). Cut-worms bother, too, but the wise grower plants enough seed to insure a stand despite the cutworms' attacks. Webworms and lice sometimes attack the leaves (see buhach, and lice remedies, in Chapter V). The corn-worm often eats the kernels of ripening corn, but no very satisfactory remedies are known. Smut (a white or black fungus) is rather common; burn diseased leaves and ears; never throw them on the manure pile.

POPCORN.—Usually grown as a farm crop, planted in hills about 3 x 3 feet apart, but may be grown in the garden the same as sweet corn, if desired. White Rice is the standard kind. Let the ears become thoroughly ripe and hard before gathering, and hang them in the attic until dry enough to pop. Do not plant popcorn near sweet corn, nor sweet corn near field corn, or the two kinds will mix.

BEANS.—All the varieties are tender and should not in the North be planted in the open ground until about May 10th (earlier farther south). First let us consider the edible-pod bush kinds known as "snap" or "string" beans. These are of two general types—the green-podded varieties (such as Stringless, Early Mohawk, Earliest Red Valentine, etc.), and the wax-podded kinds (such as Wardwell's Kidney Wax, Golden Wax, Valentine Wax, Yosemite Mammoth Wax, Stringless Wax, Perfection Wax, etc.). Sow in drills about two feet apart (two and one-half feet apart if to be worked with a horse cultivator) and cover seed not more than two inches deep. Thin the plants, when well up, to about four inches apart. Make successional sowings every two weeks, if you wish, until August 1st. Beans prefer a mellow, warm, rich soil; but do not give them too much nitrogen or they'll "run all to vines." One quart of seed will sow about 150 feet of drill. Do not cultivate or pick beans when the vines are wet, says Harriet, and I agree to that.

Snap beans for market are usually picked when about half mature, and are packed without washing in various kinds of baskets and crates. The round, one-third-barrel veneer basket is a favorite in some of the eastern states. In some localities beans can be sold in bulk to canning factories.

White navy or other beans for winter use are farm crops rather than garden crops and need not be considered here. Pole beans of the "snap" variety are listed in seed catalogs, but the bush kinds already mentioned are more handy to grow and I prefer them.

Lima beans: Plant about ten days later than snap beans. The bush limas (Burpee's, Henderson's, etc.,) should be planted in rows as advised for snap beans, but spaced about eighteen inches apart in the rows. No stakes or supports are necessary. Bush limas are best for extreme northern localities, for they do not require such a long season as the pole limas.

Pole limas (Early Leviathan and King of the Garden are good varieties) are usually planted, if in large fields, four feet apart each way (2,722 hills to the acre) and cultivated both ways so as to save considerable hand work; or the hills are often spaced three feet in four-foot-apart

PLANT ABOUT SEVEN LIMA BEANS
AROUND EACH POLE

rows, and cultivated only one way (3,630 hills to the acre). Manure and fertilizer are generally applied to each hill, and the poles are set in the center, before planting the seed. Plant about seven beans around each pole, eye downward, cover about an inch deep, and when the plants are well up thin out to about three plants to a pole. The seed is very apt to rot in the ground if soil is too wet or cold. A New Jersey bean grower informs me that he greases the beans with lard before planting, and thus prevents the rot of seed. He lards a quantity at a time in a large pan, working a little lard into the mass with his hands. One quart should plant about 100 hills.

The hills may, or may not, be raised a little above the ground level; personally I prefer them nearly level. Manure and fertilizer should be well

SETTING BEAN-POLES IN HOLES
MADE WITH A CROWBAR

mixed with soil in each hill, with a two-inch top layer of ordinary earth. Poles are preferably of cedar because that wood is so durable, but any stout pole about seven and a half feet long will do. These are easily set in holes about a foot and a half deep made with an iron crowbar (see illustration). Poles will last a long time if stored under cover in winter. When poles can not be procured, the use of braced end-posts and wires will answer the purpose and save room in a small garden. One wire should be strung about six feet high, and another about six inches from the ground—directly over the four-foot row, with the beans planted as close together as eighteen inches so as to take full advantage of this trellis system. When the beans begin to run, binder twine may be woven zigzag fashion between the two wires to form a trellis for the bean vines to climb on.

Some folks nip off the vine tips when they've reached the top of the poles or wires—to check growth and hasten the formation of beans.

Limas may be forced by starting them about a month earlier in dirt-bands, pots, etc., under glass, and then moving them to the outdoor hills about May 25th in the North, or when the second leaves are formed. (See Chapter III.) Or they may be forced in a small way in the outdoor hills, by using the box-and-glass arrangement pictured in Chapter XIII.

Marketing limas: When the shape of the beans can be distinctly seen in the pods, it is about time to pick them; of course several pickings are made at different times, until frost stops growth. Green limas are packed and shipped in their pods in various kinds of baskets, etc., or are sometimes sold at retail, shelled, by the quart.

Bean insects and diseases: The principal insect pests are the weevil (see Chapter VIII), and cutworms (Chapter XI). Several kinds of beetles sometimes eat the leaves; spraying the vines with buhach may help to discourage them, or they may be knocked into pans of kerosene. Mildew, rust and blight can be largely controlled by early sprayings with Bordeaux.

SWEET POTATOES.—For best success this crop demands a loose, sandy soil and a long, warm season;

therefore it is not grown, commercially, very far
north, although a supply for home use may be
grown almost anywhere south of central Michigan.
A very rich soil is not necessary; too much nitrogen
causes the plants to "run all to vines," but there
should be plenty of potash and phosphoric acid.

The· greater portion of the commercial crop is
grown from sets, or "draws," produced by sprouting
medium-sized potatoes in a warm bed of soil. In the
southern states the seed potatoes are sometimes cut
into pieces in the same manner as Irish potatoes and
planted in the row where they are to mature. In
the south Atlantic and Gulf Coast states the sweet
potato is frequently propagated by making vine cuttings. Where only a small area of sweet potatoes is
to be grown for home use, the necessary plants can
best be secured from some one who makes ·a business of growing them. If an acre or more is to be
planted, the grower should write to the U. S. Department of Agriculture, Washington, D. C., and get a
copy of free Farmers' Bulletin No. 324, which gives
full details impossible to give in the space at my
command.

The "ridge" method of culture is quite common.
Probably it is the best way for the small garden.
Low ridges about a foot wide are thrown up, say
three feet apart, from center to center, and are
rolled, or are allowed to settle a week or two before planting begins. The plants are set about fifteen inches apart along the center of each ridge.
Level planting is also practised, with the plants set
about thirty inches apart each way. This permits of
cultivating both ways until the vines interfere.

In the North the plants are usually set the latter
part of May or the first of June; earlier in the

South. They are very sensitive to cold. Cultivation should be thorough. The vines need disturbing to keep them from rooting at the joints.

Varieties: Yellow Nansemond and Jersey are much planted in the North. Vineless (it has shorter vines) is popular, too. These are dry and mealy-fleshed—qualities which seem to be preferred in northern kitchens. In the South the moist-fleshed, sugary tubers (often called "yams") are preferred. Southern Queen is a good one of this type.

Insects and diseases: Cutworms and flea-beetles (see Chapter XI) sometimes bother. There is also a white grub or borer which burrows in the vines or roots; infested vines should be pulled up and burned. Sweet potatoes are also subject to fungous rot, leaf-spot, scab, white rust, etc. Early sprayings with half-strength Bordeaux and rotation of crops are helps. Also the storage house, before storing tubers therein, should be fumigated with sulphur fumes.

Digging, storing and marketing: Some growers contend that sweet potatoes should be dug just before the vines are frosted. Experience proves, however, that they will keep all right if dug soon after a light frost. In the absence of a machine digger, the potatoes can be plowed out with a two-horse turning plow with a sharp rolling cutter attached to cut the vines. Or they may be dug out by hand with an ordinary potato hook. Handle as little as possible. Be careful not to bruise. Slatted bushel crates are best for handling potatoes, either sweet or Irish. If not filled level full, they can be stacked on top of each other in the wagon or elsewhere without injury to the potatoes. Only straight, smooth potatoes and none smaller than one and one-half inches should be included with those intended for market. The crooked, cut and broken potatoes, and those affected with black rot, should be saved to feed to animals.

ONE CLUSTER OF SWEETS—
WEIGHT, EIGHT POUNDS.
BE CAREFUL NOT TO
BRUISE

Pack for shipment in barrels with b u r l a p tied over the head, or in baskets, or whatever package your market prefers. The one-third-barrel, round, veneer basket lined and topped with paper, with a wooden cover, is a f a v o r i t e Maryland package for fancy "sweets." In Illinois the eleven-peck barrel lined with paper is used. If you want to store a large crop, consult Farmers' Bulletin No. 324 in regard to commercial storage methods. If you want to store a few tubers for home use, put them in ventilated crates or baskets in a *dry, warm,* frost-proof room. Do not put them in the cellar. If each tuber is wrapped in a piece of newspaper, the potatoes will keep longer. A few might be wrapped and put in paper bags and hung near the ceiling.

Remember : That it is always advantageous to grade and pack goods with care so that the quality will run uniform throughout, and then mark the contents neatly on the package. That if perishable goods come on the market late in the day they never sell so well or for so much as when in early. That the best goods sell to the best trade, and other goods to the cheap trade, and each has its level of prices.

CHAPTER XIII

CUCUMBER. MELON. PUMPKIN. SQUASH.

Plant the seeds and use the hoe,
Balmy be the weather;
Growth is sure though it be slow,
And the harvest time we'll know.

ALL of the crops mentioned in this chapter are tender and seed should not be planted in the open ground in the North until the weather is warm and settled—say about May 15th. In Georgia, I am told, the planting date would be about March 15th. A light loamy or sandy soil is best. Put a handful of complete fertilizer and a shovelful of well-rotted manure or compost in each hill, mix well with the soil and put two inches of "plain dirt" on top. I prefer low hills that are very little if any above the ground level, each hill about a foot in diameter. Sow plenty of seed—about fifteen seeds scattered all over the hill, covered half an inch deep and firmed with the back of a hoe. When the vines are well up, thin out half of them; when the remainder begin to run, thin them out so as to leave only three—well spaced. Cultivate and hoe (shallow) until the vines prevent. Some growers practise nipping off the tips of leading shoots when three or four feet in length, to force out side shoots and hasten fruiting.

These crops—especially melons and cucumbers—are oftentimes hurried along by planting the seed about a month earlier in dirt-bands, in pots, or on inverted pieces of sod (see Chapter III), and raising the plants under glass, or—on a small scale—in the kitchen window. Then, without disturbing the roots in the least, the plants are moved to hills outdoors the latter part of May when the weather is warm and settled. Or, if only a few hills are wanted, here's another way to force the plants: Sow the

A GLASS-COVERED BOX OVER EACH HILL HURRIES MELONS, ETC. PHOTO TAKEN MAY 9TH IN NEW JERSEY

seed in permanent hills outdoors early in April (in the North), and cover each hill with a small box of any kind or shape, without a bottom and with a piece of glass laid on for a top (see illustration). Thus you have a cheap, r o u g h, miniature coldframe over each hill, which serves the double purpose of raising extra-early plants, and protecting them from insects until they get so big that the boxes must be removed. A piece of mosquito-netting over the top will keep

out bugs whenever the glass is removed for ventilation (and ventilation must be closely attended to whenever the weather permits).

The foregoing general directions apply to all these vine crops. The following are additional and special points about each:

CUCUMBERS.—In large fields cucumbers for pickles are often planted in hills 5 x 5 feet apart

(1,742 to the acre), and cultivated both ways until the vines cover the ground. One ounce of seed will plant about fifty hills; about two pounds to the acre. Sowings or successional sowings may be made as late as early July in the North; in fact, pickle growers sometimes plant late on purpose—to escape the worst of the bug attack. Chicago Pickle, Everbearing, Early Frame, etc., are good pickling varieties. A small prickly kind called a gherkin is sometimes grown. The crop is gathered in burlap bags and sold by the bushel or the hundred pounds to pickle factories, who usually make contracts in advance. Only pickles of a certain specified size are wanted (usually three or four inches in length, sometimes smaller). Pickers must be hired, for the crop should be picked regularly, systematically and often; for if any of the cucumbers are allowed to grow large and mature seeds, the production of the vine soon stops (this rule applies to all cucumbers, and to some other things).

Cucumbers for table use may be planted the same as pickles, but are usually planted early because wanted early. For one-way garden culture I like to have the rows six feet apart, and hills about four feet apart in the row. White Spine is an excellent large variety. For market, cucumbers should be full size, green and not too ripe, and graded as to size. One-third-barrel round veneer baskets are often used as a shipping package in the East. (Table cucumbers are sometimes forced in greenhouses in the winter; consult Farmers' Bulletin No. 254.)

A hint for the boys: Without detaching it from the vine, slip a small cucumber into a fair-sized bottle, and after it grows so as to fill the space cut it from the vine. Folks will wonder how it got there.

Another hint: Spade up the ground in a large circle. Take a barrel, with the bottom knocked out, set it in the center of the circle and fill it two-thirds full of well-rotted manure. Plant cucumber seeds in hills around the barrel, and every day turn in upon the manure a pail or two of water. The water will soak its way through and keep the ground moist and rich.

MUSKMELONS.—Rows six feet apart and hills four feet apart in the row, are about right. E. R. Jinnette plants 5 x 5 feet and trains the vines all one way in the row to facilitate cultivating and picking. Earliness counts with this crop. Rocky Ford, Netted Gem, Osage, Paul Rose, Jenny Lind, Montreal Market, Hackensack, Blinn, etc., are favorite varieties. (NOTE: Muskmelons are often wrongly called cantaloupes. The true cantaloupe, says Prof. Bailey, is a distinct kind having a hard, warty rind; it is frequently grown in Europe, but is not much grown in this country.)

Climax baskets (one-third-bushel size with slatted cover) are a popular Illinois shipping package. A slatted crate 12 x 12 x 22¼ inches (inside measurement), holding forty-five melons each, is a well-known Colorado package. Other styles of packages are used. The fruit should be graded as to size, and packed so that the ribs of the fruit all run lengthwise of the package—this gives an attractive appearance. How to tell when a muskmelon is ripe: Only sound, heavily-netted, mature melons should be shipped. But they must not be soft nor over-ripe. *When the stem parts readily from the melon* is the right time; if not picked promptly then it soon turns yellow and soft. The vines should be picked over every day; sometimes twice a day.

WATERMELONS.—Eight by eight feet suits me for these long-running vines; some growers prefer them even farther apart. A long growing season is required, and therefore only very early varieties can be successfully grown in the North. Cole's Early is good for this purpose. In the South watermelon growing is a large industry, and carload shipments are made. Kentucky Wonder, Sweetheart, Seminole, Kolb's Gem, Gypsy, Dixie, etc., are favorite southern kinds.

There is a variety known as "citron," the rind of which is used for preserves. The flesh is not edible. The real citron of commerce comes from the fruit of a tree grown only in the far South.

The knowledge of telling a ripe watermelon comes mainly by experience and observation, says a southern grower. It is often claimed that when the little "curl" or tendril on the stem is dead, the melon is ripe; if green, the melon is also green. This is not altogether a reliable sign. The flat, dead sound emitted by the melon when thumped with the finger is also an indication of ripeness. If on turning the melon over and exposing the under side, the white blotches are found yellowish, rough, and warty, with the surface suffi-

ciently hard to resist the finger nail when scratched, it is another sign of ripeness. After the melon looks ripe and thumps as if it were ripe, and if on pressing it down, the interior appears to give, and this is also accompanied by a slight crisp crackling, the melon is almost sure to be ripe. (Melons that are to be shipped should not be put to this latter test.)

PUMPKINS.—Usually grown by farmers in corn fields. Seldom grown in the garden, but may be planted, if desired, the same as watermelons. Quaker Pie and Sugar are good varieties for home use.

SQUASH.—White Bush, Golden Custard Bush and Yellow Summer Crookneck are favorite summer kinds. Hills for these should be about four feet apart each way. Of the winter varieties, Hubbard is the best known. Marblehead, Boston Marrow, Essex Hybrid, etc., are also grown. Prize squash, etc., of extra size may be raised by leaving only one selected specimen on a vine; cut all others off and remove blossoms, nip the ends off vines, and apply liquid manure frequently to roots.

Plant winter squash the same distance apart as watermelons. Late-planted squash, I've discovered, often escape the black squash-bugs. This, and yearly rotation, are the two secrets of success. Try planting some Hubbard seed the middle of June, choosing a spot where no similar crop has been recently grown. If a few bugs do find the vines, pick off the pests in the early morning and kill them. Try covering the vines about the hills with a mound of loose earth—doing this about the time of the last cultivation, with a hoe. This will prevent the ravages of the squash root-borer which attacks the growing plants about that time, as usually the vines will start rootlets within this covering, and in spite of the injury done to their roots will grow and set nice squashes which will mature in this manner. Gather winter squash before they are frosted, and store in a dry place.

Insects and diseases: The following are enemies of all the crops mentioned in this chapter. First in importance is the well-known "striped bug" or beetle which nearly always appears as soon as the plants are above ground. In a small garden the simplest remedy is a protecting cover of mosquito-netting over each hill. In large gardens, the plants may be kept well dusted with air-slaked lime, tobacco dust and a little Paris green, mixed. Or the young plants may be sprayed with Bordeaux, adding four pounds of arsenate of lead to fifty gallons. Some growers claim that an ordinary "moth ball" placed on each hill will keep the pests away. Flea-beetles and cutworms are sometimes troublesome (see Chapter XI). Then there is a worm or caterpillar that often makes trouble; hand-picking is usually effect-ive, followed by burning old vines and rubbish, and rotation of crops. The louse or aphis often does considerable damage to the leaves and vines and is a difficult pest to combat because of its habit of hiding on the under side of the leaves. Use any of the lice remedies, and use an upward-spray noz-zle arrangement that will put the spray under the leaves (see illustration in Chapter V). The squash root-borer (see Squash) attacks other vines some-times.

Mildew, rot, blight, etc., may best be held in check with the Bordeaux mixture, beginning early and repeating the spray at intervals until the fruit is half grown. (Use half-strength Bordeaux on watermelon vines.)

THESE WATERMELONS WERE PLANTED 8 x 8 FEET APART AND THE VINES MEET; BUT THE GROWER
WISELY LEFT SEVERAL ALLEYS WIDE ENOUGH FOR A WAGON

Chapter XIV

TOMATO. EGGPLANT. PEPPER.

How these vegetables do like to be tickled with a hoe! Humor 'em often.—Farmer Vincent.

EARLY tomato plants are usually started in hotbeds in the North about February 15th. (Earlier in the South.) Refer to Chapter III for particulars of culture under glass, transplanting, etc. One ounce of seed should produce about 3,000 plants. Remember that too high a temperature and too much moisture make spindling, weak plants. Sixty-five or 70° is about right. The first transplanting to other flats in hotbeds is done about March 15th, spacing 2 x 2 inches apart. If extra-large, stocky plants are wanted, transplant them a second time, about April 15th, spacing them five inches apart, in coldframes or spent hotbeds. Finally, after well hardening-off, about the last of May the plants are moved to permanent quarters in the open ground. (Owners of small gardens will generally find it easier to buy plants than to raise them.) My late or main-crop plants are sown in hotbeds as late as April 1st, transplanted to coldframes May 1st, and set in the open ground about June 1st. They are not so large then as the earlier-grown plants, but are all right for main crop.

Outdoor rows should be four feet apart; plants

set about three feet apart in the row. Or, if you want a high, thick fence or screen (as shown in the back-yard picture on next page), the plants may be

A BARE TOWN BACK YARD. BEFORE AND—AFTER
(SEE NEXT PICTURE)

set about two feet apart and trained up on a six-foot-high netting or trellis. Large fields are sometimes set 4 x 4 feet (2,722 plants to the acre) and cultivated both ways. A light, loamy soil is best for early tomatoes. A picture on page 138 shows a gardener applying fertilizer to hills in furrows; a little rotted stable manure has previously been placed where each hill or plant is to be. This gardener afterward sets the plants over each enriched hill (his helper with a hoe first mixes soil with the hill of fertilizer and manure, puts more soil on top, and makes an opening for the plant). After each plant is set the soil is firmly trodden around it with the feet; the furrow, between hills, is either filled with the hoe as the planting progresses, or the filling is done by cultivating crosswise after the entire field is set.

The after cultivation should be thorough and regular. When the vines are large enough to need support they should be tied loosely to stakes about

four feet high (higher, if desired), or supported on
high wire or wooden trellises, or on low Λ-shaped
frames or racks, or on piles of brush placed beneath
the vines—in fact, anything will answer that will keep
them off the ground. (Where large areas of tomatoes are grown the vines are seldom supported.)
Pinching off the tips of the main upper shoots when
the plants on racks are about three feet high is prac-

SAME BACK YARD AFTER GROWING FLOWERS,
VINES AND A HIGH SCREEN OF TOMATOES

tised by a few gardeners, who claim that it "makes
the fruit earlier and finer"; some others train the
vines to long stakes and regularly pinch off the side
shoots; many others do no pruning of any kind.

Varieties of tomatoes: Earliana, Atlantic Prize,
Chalk's Early Jewel, Matchless, etc., are well-known
early red kinds, the first-named being especially early,
I find. Stone, Acme, Perfection, Jersey Red, Matchless, Beauty, etc., are good main-crop varieties. Tomato varieties soon "run out" and new kinds are
constantly being introduced; so names change

quickly. "Peach," Yellow "Plum," Red "Cherry,"
"Husk" and similar tomatoes are sometimes grown
for preserves or as novelties.

Marketing Tomatoes: Gathering should be done
two or three times a week—sometimes every day—
only picking the fruits that are ready each time. If
to be shipped some distance, pick them when they are
just beginning to color—even sooner for very long
distances. For near-by market let them color all
over, or nearly so, on the vines, but they should not
be over-ripe and soft. Choice early tomatoes for

APPLYING FERTILIZER TO MANURED
HILLS IN FURROWS, FOR TOMA-
TOES (SEE PAGE 136)

distant shipment are
usually p a c k e d in
crates h o l d i n g six
baskets (similar to a
Georgia peach crate),
and each tomato is
wrapped in paper. Or
sometimes flat boxes
carrying two layers
of wrapped fruits are
used. Later tomatoes
from near-by points
are packed in a variety of packages—bushel crates,
half-bushel baskets, third-barrel baskets, etc. Tomatoes for canning factories are best handled in the
slatted bushel boxes recommended for potatoes; the
factories contract to pay a certain price "per ton."

If frost threatens before the tomatoes and peppers are all gathered, says Harriet (leaning over my
shoulder as I write), cover them with cloths or
papers and save them; or pull the plants and hang
them under a shed; or cover with straw where they
stand; or pick the larger green tomatoes and let
them ripen in the sun indoors; or wrap each green

tomato in paper, store in a cool cellar, and keep for later ripening in the sun.

Insects and diseases: The large green tomato worm is the principal insect pest. Spray young plants with arsenate of lead; hand-pick the worms on fruiting vines. Rot and blight are the chief diseases. Practise rotation of crops; burn all diseased fruit and dead vines; keep the vines off the ground; spray with the Bordeaux mixture, beginning early and continuing at intervals until a few weeks before picking time.

EGGPLANT.—The plants are grown under glass the same as tomatoes, except that they require more heat and care in the hotbed, and need not be started quite so early. March 1st is soon enough, in the North. One hotbed transplanting is sufficient if you space the plants well apart. To reach maturity, a long, warm season is required; therefore commercial success with this crop can not be expected too far north. Choose a rich, loose, loamy soil; clay is not so suitable; neither is too wet a soil. New York Improved, Black Beauty and Black Pekin are the best varieties where the season is long enough; in extreme northern localities the Early Dwarf Purple would be more apt to mature its fruit. Plants may be set 2½ x 2½ feet outdoors about June 1st in the North; this is for hoe cultivation. For horse work in a large field, 3 x 3 feet would be better.

Marketing eggplant: The fruit is usually cut from the stem when nearly full-grown and fully-colored. An over-ripe fruit changes from a bright to a dull purple, and the seeds inside begin to swell; it is then worthless for market or table use. Gathering the fruits before they quite reach full size increases the crop. A marketable eggplant should be from six to nine inches long. Wipe clean, sort as to size, and pack in barrels, baskets or crates.

Diseases and insects: Anthracnose (pinkish pits or spots on the fruit), rot, mold, leaf-spot and stem-blight are best prevented and held in check by early and regular sprayings with the Bordeaux mixture. Flea-beetles, potato bugs, etc., often attack the vines (see remedies elsewhere).

PEPPERS.—The mild, sweet varieties for slicing or stuffing are mostly in demand—such as Ruby King, Bull Nose, Sweet Mountain, Chinese Giant, Neapolitan, etc. Long Red Cayenne is the hot pepper of commerce; Chili and Cranberry are pickling favorites. Grow plants in hotbeds the same as eggplant. Set outdoors late in May, in rows two and one-half feet apart, plants spaced twenty inches apart in the row. Marketing may begin when the peppers are a little more than half grown, and may continue until they are ripe. Open barrels, crates, baskets, etc., are used, each variety or size of pepper being kept by itself. Unlike eggplant or tomatoes, peppers often endure a small degree of frost in the fall (although while young the plants are very tender). Pepper plants are seldom troubled with insects; anthracnose and rot are the most common diseases (see Eggplant).

FIGHTING FROST.—Commercial truckers sometimes save their tender vegetables, melons, etc., from untimely late-May or early-fall frosts, by lighting smudge fires here and there throughout the patch.

Chapter XV

MISCELLANEOUS

Artichoke, Celeriac, Chard, Corn Salad, Cress, Endive, Ginseng, Herbs, Leek, Mushroom, Mustard, Okra, Parsley, Spinach, etc.

THERE are two distinct kinds of artichokes—one is grown for its potato-like, underground tubers and is called Jerusalem artichoke, and the other is called the Globe artichoke and the parts eaten are the unopened flower heads (and sometimes the young shoots). The former kind is seldom grown in American gardens, being considered more suited for farm culture for stock food; perfectly hardy; multiplies rapidly and will become a bad weed if not kept within bounds; once planted it will maintain itself indefinitely; plant the tubers the same distance apart as you would potatoes. The Globe artichoke is propagated by seeds, or by suckers taken from other plants. Seeds do not grow true to name. Seedsmen sell plants for about $1.50 per dozen. Set them about 3 x 3 feet apart; protect the crowns in winter with straw, etc.; plants are good for about three years; not often grown in this country, but worth growing.

CELERIAC.—Little known in the United States. It is a turnip-rooted kind of celery, and the "turnip" is the edible part—either cooked or as a salad.

Grown about the same as celery, but the stalks are not blanched; the turnip part can be stored in winter the same as any other root crop.

CHARD.—Also called Swiss chard or "leaf beet." Few Americans know or value this member of the beet family, but Harriet and I have recently learned to prize it highly. Be sure to try some, early next spring. Sow the seed in rows about two feet apart and thin the plants so they'll stand about fifteen inches apart in the row. The thinnings may be used for "greens." When the plants are full-grown the large leaves and stalks may be pulled as wanted (about as you pull rhubarb). Sometimes Harriet cuts up and cooks leaves and stalks together (as you would spinach); sometimes she cooks the whitish stalk part just as if it were asparagus, and uses only the leaves for "greens." Either way, the result is surprisingly pleasing. We like the greens better than spinach. The plants produce stalks and leaves until fall. Must be planted each year. Easy to grow.

CORN SALAD.—Hardy. Sow in early spring the same as lettuce. It matures in about seven weeks and furnishes a bunch of leaves for salad. Or may be sown late in summer for fall use. Seldom grown in this country.

CRESS.—There are two well-known kinds—"water cress," and "garden cress." (There is a third kind, called "upland cress," which is little known.) Water cress is a perennial and does best in moist places or in running water. Seed may be purchased of seedsmen and scattered along the edges of brooks, etc. It grows without care when once established. It may also be propagated by planting pieces of plant stems in the wet earth. Garden cress is an annual, nearly hardy, and may be sown in April in the garden like lettuce, or in late summer for fall use. Water cress is the kind usually seen in markets, being better known than the garden variety.

ENDIVE.—Henry A. Dreer says: "Endive is one of the best and most wholesome salads for fall and winter use. Sow in shallow drills in April for early use; or for late use sow in June or July. When three inches high, transplant or thin out to one foot apart. When nearly full grown, and before they are fit for the table, the plants must be bleached. This is done by gathering the leaves together and tying, to exclude the light and air from the inner leaves, which must be done when quite dry, or they will rot. Another method is to cover the plants with boards or slats. In three or four weeks they will be blanched."

GINSENG.—A hardy perennial plant found growing wild in shady places in many parts of the country, the roots of which are prized for medicinal purposes by the Chinese. Seeds are planted in the fall but usually do not germinate for eighteen months, and not at all if not expertly handled; therefore most gardeners who want to grow ginseng buy young plants or roots of some professional grower. The roots grow slowly, and five or six years must elapse before they are large enough to gather. A sandy-loam soil and partial shade are best.

Some folks seem to see a big future for cultivated ginseng; but personal observation and inquiry have made me a little sceptical about it. I can not advise my readers to invest heavily in the business nor to build rosy air-castles on possible profits. The Chinese are the only buyers of the dried roots, and the commercial possibilities of the business are therefore limited. I hear, too, that Chinese buyers discriminate in favor of the wild root, paying a less price for the cultivated product. Altogether it looks to me as if the market might easily be glutted—and then what? If you want to make money, better let fads alone and stick to the staple products that everybody wants. For further information write to the U. S. Department of Agriculture and ask for bulletins on the subject of ginseng growing.

HERBS.—These are of three kinds—pot herbs for flavoring, sweet herbs and medicinal herbs. It is a great pity that herbs are now seldom raised in the home garden. The use of them in medicine is perhaps not so great in these days when a doctor can be readily called, but in the old times no housewife was without a goodly show of them in the yard, and she dried them carefully for winter use. Nor are herbs used nowadays so much for flavoring in cooking; and, when they are desired, the pressed leaves are

PUTTING AWAY HERBS FOR WINTER USE

bought at the druggist's. The home-grown article is far better than money can buy. A home with even a small strip of land can find place for some of these plants which are so valuable.

Herbs delight in a rich, mellow soil. Put them in a corner by themselves where they will not interfere with plowing, etc. When once started, little if any cultivation is needed except to keep out weeds. Sow seeds early in spring in shallow drills about two feet apart; when up a few inches thin out to a foot or more apart. Herbs should be cut on a dry day just before they come into full blossom, tied in bunches and hung up in the attic or spread thinly on a floor where they can dry quickly. Of course cuttings for daily use, green, may be made at any time, but too severe cutting weakens the plants. Seedsmen sell plants, ready to set, of some of the better-known herbs. Many of the perennial kinds may be propagated by dividing the roots—which is a good thing to do every few years; and, when doing so, discard the old, run-out part of each clump.

Among the better-known perennial herbs are the following: Balm, catnip, fennel, horehound, hyssop, lavender (not hardy too far north), sweet marjoram, pennyroyal, peppermint, rosemary, rue, sage, spearmint, tansy, tarragon, thyme, winter savory, wormwood. Anise, coriander, summer savory and sweet basil are annuals. Caraway and dill are biennials. A winter mulch of straw or leaves is a good thing for the perennial herbs.

LEEK.—Used in cooking, as a seasoning. Milder than the onion. Sow early in April, in drills one foot apart and one inch deep. When plants are six inches high, transplant in a deep, rich soil, in rows twelve inches apart and six inches in the rows, as deep as possible, so that the neck may be covered and blanched; draw the earth to them as they grow. The seed may also be sown in August or September and plants transplanted in the spring. The thick leaves, as well as the soft bulb, are used. Leeks may be stored green, with the roots in moist earth, in a cool cellar.

MUSHROOM.—The growing of mushrooms in cellars, sheds, etc., is sometimes called a fad, but—unlike ginseng culture—it has substantial American market possibilities. There is a steadily-growing demand for good, fresh mushrooms, and I believe that expert growers, properly equipped, can make money in the business. But, like everything else that promises so well, it "isn't so easy as it looks." Amateurs should not expect to pick up many dollars until they have acquired the necessary experience and "knack." The culture of mushrooms is not, strictly speaking, within the scope of a garden book, and therefore I have not room to go into details; but any reader who is interested in the subject can get full information by writing to the U. S. Department of Agriculture, Washington, D. C., and asking for free Farmers' Bulletin No. 204.

MUSTARD.—Some people grow this for salads. The seeds are often used for flavoring pickles, etc. For salads, sow thickly in shallow drills, about a foot apart, in April. Successive sowings may be made every week or two. To grow seed, thin out to four inches apart when two inches high.

OKRA.—More grown in the South than in the North. Often called "Gumbo." The dwarf varieties are best for northern gardeners. This vegetable is extensively grown for its green pods, which are used in soups, stews, etc., to which they impart a rich flavor, and are considered nutritious. Sow the seed thickly in rich, warm ground about the last of May (in the North), in drills three feet apart, one inch deep; thin to one foot apart.

PARSLEY.—A hardy biennial plant much used for garnishing and seasoning soups, meats, etc. Sow thickly early in April in rows one foot apart and one-half inch deep; thin out the plants to stand six inches apart in the rows. The seed germinates very slowly and often fails to come up in dry weather. To assist its coming up quicker, soak the seed. For winter use protect in a coldframe or in a light cellar.

SPINACH.—For spring and summer use in the North, sow the seed either broadcast, or in drills one foot apart and one inch deep, as early as the ground can be worked, and every two weeks for a succession. For winter and early spring use, sow in September in well-manured ground; cover with straw or leaves on the approach of severe weather. The richer the ground, the more succulent will be the leaves. For wintering, sow only the hardy, prickly variety. Long-Standing and Victoria are good kinds for summer use. (The large New Zealand variety should be sown in hills 3 x 3 feet apart, four seeds to a hill.)

Cardoon, chervil, chicory, chives, dandelion, garlic, sorrel, etc., are listed in seedsmen's catalogs, but are so seldom grown in American gardens that detailed information about them seems unnecessary here.

ENTRANCE TO A GARDEN. NOTE THE NEATLY-CLIPPED PRIVET
HEDGES AND SMALL EVERGREENS, AND THE ARCH OF
CRIMSON RAMBLER ROSES

Chapter XVI

THE FLOWER GARDEN

The man who cheerfully sets the spade where his wife directs, and lends himself willingly to her desires in the flower garden, has in him the vital elements of good citizenship and is a safe man to trust.—Tim.

OH, for the return of the old-fashioned flower garden! Years ago flowers were grown in borders rather than in beds—box-edged borders on each side of a rear walk, or alongside a fence or a wall or a building, filled with a profusion of old-time favorites growing in a delightfully informal mass of color and variety. In those days the nightmare "beds" (dug out of the lawn in round or fanciful shapes) filled with geraniums or foliage plants (set straight and exactly even all around), were not common.

George H. Ellwanger, in The Garden's Story, touches a tender spot in my heart when he says:

"One passes many neglected farm-gardens along the road. Here, an old locust and mock-orange have been allowed to sprout at will: the blue iris has crept outside the fence, with clumps of double daffodils turned over by the plow and flung on to the roadside. There is a jungle of stunted quinces and blighted pear trees. The spreading myrtle patch has usurped the place of what was once a lawn; tall thistles, hog-weed, pig-weed and burdocks make and scatter seed year after year; an army of weeds has overrun the path—the plantain, purslane, goose-grass, dandelion, joint-weed and mallow; and a green goose-pond, over which are hovering yellow butterflies, exhales its miasma in the sun. Once the garden was beautiful, famous for its old-fashioned flowers, and many were the slips the neighbors obtained from its floral stores. The grain-fields and fat pastures corresponded with the luxuriance within. But the farm changed hands on the death of the owner, and the new owners cared little for the flowers."

In the hope that my readers may be induced to reclaim the old gardens or start new ones along the old lines, I will give a condensed and partial list of the plants, etc., that Harriet and I (and some of the friends whom we've consulted) think should be included in an old-fashioned flower border:

Hardy Perennial Plants and Bulbs

Anemone Japonica (also called Japanese anemone): Grows two or three feet high. Blooms from August until frost. Needs slight protection in winter in extreme North. White or pink varieties may be had.

Bachelor's Buttons (sometimes called "double buttercup"): Grows about a foot and a half high, and produces double yellow flowers in May and June. Prefers wet soil.

Bergamot: Aromatic and sweet-scented; produces a profusion of showy bloom from July until frost. Grows about two feet high. White, pink, purple or scarlet varieties.

Bleeding-heart (dicentra): An old-time favorite. Bears heart-shaped flowers in graceful, drooping, reddish racemes, in April, May and June. Fern-like foliage about two feet high.

Campanula (Canterbury bells; bellflower) : About two feet high. Attractive blue or white flowers in early summer. Calycanthema (cup-and-saucer) is a favorite variety.

Candytuft (evergreen or hardy candytuft) : A low-growing plant suitable for the foreground of borders. White flowers in early spring.

Cardinal Flower (lobelia cardinalis) : Blooms in spikes of brilliant cardinal-red, in August. Plants about one and a half feet high.

Chrysanthemum, Hardy: Grows about two feet high. Several varieties and colors. Flowers in late summer and until frost.

Columbine: Height, one to three feet—according to variety. White, red, yellow, etc. April-June; some varieties later. Succeeds in almost any soil.

Coreopsis: Blooms June-September. Height about one and a half feet. Lanceolata grandiflora is a popular variety. Yellow.

Crocus: Fine for early-spring bloom. Plant the bulbs about October first in the North, in fine, rich, deep, well-drained soil. Mulch with a little strawy manure, or leaves, or straw alone. Remove mulch in early spring. Divide and transplant the bulbs every three or four years. Plant crocus bulbs about three inches deep; about four inches apart, irregularly—I do not fancy things too straight in the flower border.

Daffodils, Jonquils and Poet's Narcissus are planted and divided the same as crocuses; but set them about an inch deeper and about two inches farther apart.

Day Lily: The best yellow variety is Hemero-

callis flava. Grows about two feet high. Blooms in
June.

Ferns: A few, here and there, help the general
effect.

Flag (blue flag; iris): Since the blue flag of
our grandmothers' time, the iris has been improved
and new kinds introduced until now there is a nice
list of beauties of different tints and colors—the
Japanese iris, the German iris, etc. And varieties
may be had which bloom at different times, prolong-
ing the season from May to July. Buy one or more
"clumps," of seedsmen, set them out in the fall,
mulch through the winter, and "watch 'em grow and
spread." If they eventually crowd out of bounds,
cut off the outer parts of the clumps with a spade,
and set the detached slices of roots elsewhere.

Forget-me-not: A low-growing plant. Blue
flowers. April-May.

Foxglove: Various varieties and colors. June-
July. Plants about two and one-half feet high.

Funkia (plantain lily): Foliage and flowers
both attractive. Many varieties and colors. Blooms
July-August. Plants about a foot and a half high.

Grasses: Clumps of the various ornamental
grasses might well be included in the back corners
of the border. Their leaves are almost as striking
as some flowers.

Harebell (bluebells of Scotland): A dwarf-
growing species of campanula; only about a foot
high.

Hibiscus (marshmallow): Grows about five
feet high. Blooms August-September. Large,
showy, pink flowers. (Meehan's Mallow Marvel is
a recent introduction of distinct and superior merit.
The plants grow as high as a man and I never saw

more gorgeous pink, red, white, etc., flowers. Be
sure to plant some of these.)

Hollyhock: A general favorite. Single or
double varieties. Height about six feet. Various
colors. June-August. They like a deep, rich soil,
and appreciate a mulch-protection in the winter. A
fungous disease often attacks them, but early sprayings with the Bordeaux mixture should prevent it.

Hyacinth: Fine for early spring bloom. Various
colors. Plant and treat the bulbs the same as advised
for daffodils, but set them an inch deeper.

Jacob's Ladder: Handsome foliage and spikes of
blue flowers. June-July. Grows about a foot high.

Larkspur: Great spikes of bloom (various
colors) produced continuously from June until late
summer. The tall kinds attain a height of five feet
or more; dwarf varieties about two feet.

Lily: I could write a chapter about these, but,
alas! space forbids. Among the many excellent
varieties I can mention
the following: Lilium
candidum—white, blooms
in June, often grows six
feet high, s o m e t i m e s
called "annunciation lily";
lilium auratum, about three
feet high, blooms July-
August, also called "gold-
banded lily of Japan";
l i l i u m longiflorum, or
"trumpet lily," white, two
and one-half feet high,

LILY-OF-THE-VALLEY—A GREAT
FAVORITE OF HARRIET'S

June; lilium tigrinum splendens, or "tiger lily,"
spotted orange color, four feet high, August; lily-
of-the-valley is last but not least—a home is incom-

plete without a clump of these lowly little beauties. Plant lily bulbs in early October the same as advised for crocus and other hardy bulbs, but be sure to spade up the soil *deeply;* cover about six inches deep, space about fifteen inches apart, and apply a winter mulch. Lily-of-the-valley "pips" need not be covered deeper than about three inches. Divide and transplant lilies every three or four years.

Monk's-hood: Likes a shady place. Blooms August-September. The old variety has a blue flower and grows to a height of about three feet.

Myrtle: A well-known evergreen trailing plant with blue flowers in spring. Does well almost anywhere and spreads rapidly.

Pæony: There are two distinct types—the ordinary herbaceous pæony and the "tree" pæony. Both types come in a variety of colors—pink, white, red, etc.,—and the blooming time may be greatly extended by getting early and late kinds. Set the plants in the fall in deep, rich, well-drained soil; space at least two and one-half feet apart (farther for tree pæonies); mulch in winter.

Passion Flower: A trailing blue flower that blooms July-September.

Phlox, Hardy: Assorted colors and heights, according to variety. Phloxes are among the very showiest and most valuable of all hardy plants, and by growing a complete collection they can be had in bloom from early June until late fall. The old lilac and purple-colored varieties have given way to the beautiful hybrid sorts of handsome and brilliant shades of pink, red, salmon, rose, in distinct colors. They form large clumps and should be in every garden, as they succeed in almost any position with little care.

Pink: Delightful low-growing flowers. Who doesn't remember the "moss" or "mountain" or "clove" pink of his boyhood days? Then there is the newer white variety called Her Majesty.

Poppy: Many people do not know that the Iceland and the Oriental varieties are hardy perennials, and quite unlike the Shirley or annual kinds. Sow the seed in the *fall* in finely prepared ground, mulch lightly, remove the mulch in the spring—and await developments, says Harriet.

Pyrethrum: Daisy-like flowers of various colors. Two feet.

Rudbeckia: The variety called Golden Glow is the most popular nowadays (and it is indeed a glow of yellow for sometime in the summer). Grows six feet high. Be sure to have some.

Snowdrop (anemone or windflower): Plant the same as crocus bulbs.

Spiderwort: An old favorite. Flowers violet-blue. June-August. About two feet in height. There is a white variety which is not so well known.

Starworts (hardy aster or Michaelmas daisy): Desirable additions to the garden, because the different varieties bloom late when few hardy plants are in flower. Various colors and heights.

Sunflower: Plant a few of the hardy, perennial kinds, at the back of the border. Try Multiflorus, Maximus, Major and Soleil d' Or.

Sweet-william: A great favorite. About a foot high. Various colors. May-June.

Tulip: Plant and treat the same as daffodils. It is not necessary to take up the bulbs every year, although an occasional dividing and transplanting is desirable. After the flowers and leaves die down, remove them in early summer and—if you wish—stir the soil lightly and sow flower seed of some kind, so that the ground may be occupied without disturbing the bulbs beneath.

Violet, Sweet: Partial shade is acceptable. Be sure to save a place for these blue beauties. (Nowadays some folks make money by growing them under glass in frames or greenhouses, and selling the product in the larger towns and cities; the California variety is also largely grown.)

Yucca (Spanish bayonet or Adam's needle): An evergreen plant somewhat resembling a century plant. Flowers borne in spikes on tall flower-stalks. June-July.

GENERAL REMARKS AND CULTURAL HINTS.— Numerous additions might be made to the foregoing list, but the varieties mentioned will serve as an excellent beginning and the flower-lover can try other kinds from time to time. (There's always room for "one more" in an informal border, says Martha.) In regard to planting and culture, many of the varieties may be grown from seed in seedbeds outdoors or in window-boxes indoors, and transplanted to the border when ready; or they may be sown in their permanent places and thinned out when well up. Or plants or bulbs may be purchased of seedsmen, thus saving time and bother. Plants all ready to set are sold very cheap. Distances apart need not be exactly considered, for straight rows are to be avoided in the border; simply have the plants so they do not unduly crowd each other, and thin them out from time to time as their growth may require. Have the low-growing kinds toward the front edge, the medium growers in the middle, and the tall varieties at the rear. The flower colors should be arranged in a pleasing way—as if you were painting a picture or composing a harmony. Avoid glaring contrasts, abrupt, straight divisions, and jarring combinations; you can not expect to get everything right at first, but some plants can be reset if necessary until the desired effect is secured (even large plants can be safely moved in late fall). Keep out weeds, keep the soil loose and mellow; but when the plants have attained sufficient size to cover and shade the ground, few weeds will grow and only an occasional hoeing or weeding will be necessary. Late each fall apply a mulch of strawy manure and a light sprinkle of bone meal; remove the c o a r s e r parts of the mulch in the early spring and carefully loosen up the surface soil with a hoe and a n a r r o w eight-tooth rake.

REMOVE THE MULCH IN EARLY SPRING AND CAREFULLY LOOSEN UP THE TOP SOIL

Prepare the border for planting by spading it deeply (a foot at least) and working in a quantity of well-rotted manure and some bone meal. Most of the seeds can best be sown in spring as soon as the ground is warm and dry enough—say late April or early May in the North; a few of them (poppies, for instance) can best be sown in late fall and mulched. In regard to buying and setting out plants, J. T. Lovett says: "Some persons prefer autumn planting and others claim spring to be the better season. As a matter of fact, neither spring nor fall is to be preferred for the entire list of varieties. Beyond question pæony, phlox, dicentra, day lily, etc., make the best growth when planted in autumn; while Japanese anemone, foxglove, Canterbury bells, hollyhock, sweet-william and some others frequently perish the first winter if planted in the fall—though they are per-fectly hardy after they become well established in their new homes."

The heights of the various plants and the time of flowering, as given, are of course only approxi-mate—much depends upon climate, soil and season, and therefore exact statements are impossible. One of the advantages of having a border planted only to hardy perennials, is that it need be planted but once; thus the annual "fuss" with seeds, and the un-certainty, is avoided.

FLOWERING SHRUBS.—Somewhere in the garden there should be at least a few of the hardy shrubs, to supplement the perennial plants already mentioned. They may be set along the back line of the flower border; or may be set in a border or bed by them-selves, putting the tall-growing kinds to the rear (or center) and the lower kinds in front. (Distances apart vary from two to four or five or six feet, ac-cording to variety.) Here is a short suggestive list of shrubs: Althea (high-growing, late-blooming); azalea (hardy kinds, low, early); barberry (Thun-bergi is best-known variety, low, red berries); deut-zia (both dwarf and tall-growing kinds, June); for-sythia (golden flowers very early, medium height); hydrangea paniculata grandiflora (splendid late bloomer, plant in masses, prune new wood closely each year, attains good size in time); lilac (high, early, several varieties); rhododendron (prefers shade, different sizes and colors, not hardy too far north, requires no pruning); snowball (an old-time favorite, high, early); spirea (various kinds, heights and colors—plant several); sweet-scented shrub (a favorite of our grandmothers', fragrant chocolate-colored flowers) ; syringa or mock-orange (high, early) ; weigela (mid-season or early summer, high).

Pruning and care of shrubs: Keep the surface of the ground loose and mellow. Mulch with strawy manure in fall. Prune early-blooming shrubs *as soon as bloom has ceased;* prune late bloomers early the following spring. Little if any pruning is needed the first few years, but the shrubs should be well "cut back" at time of setting. There is no particular science about pruning shrubs, other than the points already mentioned; simply thin out, trim up or cut back, as taste or circumstances may require.

ROSES.—No garden is quite complete without a rose bed. I have not space to mention the many excellent varieties here, but be sure to plant some of the hybrid perpetuals (Baroness Rothschild, pink; Captain Hayward, carmine; General Jacqueminot, crimson; Margaret Dickson, white; Marshall P. Wilder, carmine; Mrs. John Laing, pink; Paul Neyron, deep rose color; Ulrich Brunner, cherry red, are among the most satisfactory kinds). Hybrid perpetuals are quite hardy nearly everywhere, but a heavy mulch of leaves or straw through the winter is always helpful. Although called "perpetuals," they are not really perpetual bloomers; but many of them will produce a fair second-crop of flowers in the autumn.

The hybrid-tea roses are more tender, but are all-season bloomers if well cared for. In the North, bend the branches down to the ground and stake them there in late autumn and apply stable manure, and on top of that a thick covering of straw or leaves, held securely against winds by wire chicken-netting laid flat and fastened along the edges with stakes. Remove the covering about May 1st. Good varieties are: Caroline Testout, bright rose color; Gruss an Teplitz, scarlet; Kaiserin Augusta Victoria, creamy white; Killarney, one of the most beautiful pink roses in existence; La France, silvery pink, very attractive.

Tea roses are very free-flowering, but are almost too tender for growing outdoors in the North, even if protected with straw. In the greenhouse or in the South, they are fine.

Then there are those old favorites, the moss roses and the sweetbriars. The Rugosa roses, of Japanese origin, are hardy and interesting; the seed-pods are quite ornamental. Wichuriana is a low-trailing species producing white flowers in July after the June roses are through blooming (Dorothy Perkins is of the same species, but the flowers are pink). The dwarf Polyantha roses bear pleasing clusters of dainty small flowers.

Pruning, culture and rose-bugs: Cut off the upper one-third of each main shoot in the spring; cut out all dead or diseased wood at any time; ever-blooming roses may be cut back again after the June flowering, which induces further bloom. Keep the ground well stirred all through the growing season; spade deeply before planting; set plants about two feet apart (more or less according to variety); remember that roses like a very rich clay-loam soil with sufficient moisture. Rose-bugs are the worst pest, generally, and no very good remedies are known. Cover the bushes with mosquito-netting, or knock the bugs into a pan of kerosene twice a day, or spray with arsenate of lead as suggested in Chapter V. (For other enemies, see general remarks and hints on pages 166 and 167.)

CLIMBING VINES.—These as a rule do not belong in the border, but should find a place somewhere in or near the garden—on porch, house, wall, lattice screen, or climbing upon a dead tree-trunk, post or fence. Crimson Rambler, Prairie Queen, Baltimore Belle, etc., are hardy climbing roses that succeed almost everywhere (give slight protection the first two years in extreme northern localities, by laying the vines down and covering during the winter; older vines seem quite hardy; no protection necessary at any time in Philadelphia). Boston ivy, Virginia creeper, English ivy, trumpet flower, honeysuckles of various kinds, wistaria and clematis are all good in their proper places. The flowers of clematis paniculata and

ENTRANCE TO A LONG ISLAND GAR-
DEN.   ARBOR COVERED WITH CLEM-
ATIS PANICULATA, ETC.

clematis Jackmani are especially attractive. Little if any pruning is necessary, except to cut out dead or diseased wood at any time, and to remove surplus or not-wanted growth in the spring. Cultivate a circle of ground around the roots, and mulch with stable manure. English ivy is not hardy in the extreme North, but the others will do well nearly everywhere if laid down and protected the first two years.

ANNUAL PLANTS AND VINES.—Planting flower seed every year is a bother, but flower lovers can not quite get along without some of their favorite one-season bloomers. I can only mention a few of the best-known:

Aster: The various annual varieties permit of a blooming season from July until frost. Sow seed in window boxes in early spring and transplant in May; or sow the earlier kinds outdoors in late April.

Canna: Not easy to grow from seed (see hints under Moonflower). Better buy roots of a seedsman. Set in rich, moist soil about fifteen inches apart May 15th, or when danger of frost is over. In the fall after a heavy frost, cut off tops near the ground; later, before ground freezes, dig roots, dry them well in the sun, and store in a cool cellar. The roots need dividing every year or so.

Dahlia: May be grown from seed, but most people prefer to buy roots of a seedsman and plant out about May 15th, or when the weather is warm and settled. Earlier bloom may be secured by starting the roots in boxes in the house three weeks ahead of outdoor planting time. Tie the plants to stakes, for support. Have the ground rich. When frost threatens in the fall, cover the plants with cloths or papers at night and thus prolong the blooming season until late. After frost has blackened the vines, cut them off near the ground. Dig the roots on a sunny day, dry them well, and store in a cool cellar. The roots may be divided from time to time, and the surplus used or sold. (Divide with a sharp knife; see that a part of old stem, with a bud, is attached to each tuber.)

Gladiolus: Plant the bulbs in late April about three inches deep and six inches apart. The flower stalks often need some support. Successive plantings may be made until July 1st, if a long season of bloom is desired. After frost comes, dig the bulbs, and when well dried in the sun cut off each stalk about six inches above the bulb; store in a *dry,* frost-proof place. The bulbs increase rapidly each year.

Marigold: The African varieties grow about two feet high and bear large yellow or orange-colored flowers; the French kinds are more dwarf in habit, usually with striped colors. Raise plants indoors or in frames in early spring and transplant to open ground in May; or sow seed outdoors in late April.

Moonflower: Large white flowers opening in the evening. A strong climber. Best to start seeds in the house in March and transplant in May, or buy plants of a seedsman. The seeds germinate slowly and uncertainly. File or cut a small notch through the hard coat or shell of each seed, keeping away from the germinating point, and the seeds will sprout more quickly. (This hint also applies to canna or other large hard seeds.)

Morning-glory: A climbing favorite. Sow as early as possible in the spring, and give the vines something to run on. Or sow the seed in well-prepared ground in the fall and mulch through the winter. The Imperial Japanese kinds are larger and finer colored.

Nasturtium: There are dwarf varieties and tall or climbing kinds. They like a well-drained, sunny place, and will blossom until frost comes. Usually sown outdoors in late April, but may be started earlier in the house and transplanted outside in May.

Pansy: Does well in partial shade or in a sunny situation. For very early spring flowering the seed may be sown in coldframes in autumn; or in the open ground, plants well protected with straw or leaves through the winter; or sow seed indoors in March and transplant to the open ground in April.

For summer blooming, sow seed outdoors in April.
Pick the flowers often, so that none will go to seed.
Seed production soon stops bloom.

Pea, Sweet: Likes a deep, heavy loam. Sow
in *early* spring in drills about five inches deep; cover
only about three inches deep at first, filling in the
remaining three inches when the plants are just
coming through the first covering. May also be
sown in fall and mulched. Support the vines on
wire-netting, brush, etc. Pick the flowers often;
allow none to go to seed—this is important if you
want a long blooming season. In regard to insects
and fungi, consult Chapter VIII.

Petunia: The double petunias are handsome,
but the single kinds are entirely satisfactory. I
usually sow the seed outdoors in late April and thin
the plants to about ten inches apart; however, earlier
bloom may be had by starting the plants in window
boxes indoors and transplanting them in May.

Phlox Drummondi: This is one of Harriet's
favorite annuals. She likes to have a solid mass of
it somewhere, composed of separate white, crimson,
pink and yellow kinds; this gives a better effect than
the ordinary mixtures sold. (The same rule holds
true with sweet peas and some other flowers; buy
and plant each color by itself and the result is more
pleasing.) Grow the same as petunias.

Tuberose: Cut away the dead roots and set the
bulbs in deep, rich soil in late May or when all danger of frost is over. Put about an inch of soil over
the tops of the bulbs. Just before frost in the fall,
dig up the bulbs and cut off the tops so as to leave
about two inches of stem attached to each bulb.
Place in shallow boxes and dry for a week in the
sun, protecting on cool nights; then store away in a

dry, frost-proof place until the following spring. The little new bulbs or "pips" which grow on the older bulbs should be detached and planted separately; they will bloom the second year.

Verbena: For best results, sow seed in window boxes or hotbeds in early spring and transplant to the open ground in May.

Zinnia: Grown in the same manner as petunias.

Then there are a host of other annuals—candytuft, cosmos, gillyflower or stock, lady-slipper, mignonette, portulaca, Shirley and California poppies, sweet alyssum, etc., etc.,—which I have not room to touch upon here. But they are nearly all of easy culture and the grower needs no special knowledge.

As for the many kinds of so-called "house plants" that are often moved in pots to the garden in summer time, I can only say: Beware of setting them out too early; toughen them first by letting them stand on a sheltered porch for a few days, protecting them with newspapers or cloths during cold nights. Boston ferns and other house ferns are improved by sinking the pots to the brim in the ground in a place outdoors sheltered from hard winds and partially or wholly shaded; thus treated (and occasionally sprinkled with water) they will "renew their beauty" for another winter.

INSECT AND FUNGOUS ENEMIES.—Only a few general remarks are possible here. A careful study of Chapter V should help the flower grower to decide upon a remedy for almost any trouble. Does the insect *eat?* Then arsenate of lead, hellebore, etc., will kill it. Or, if it does not eat foliage or flowers, mustn't it *suck* the juices from leaf or branch by inserting its beak inside where stomach poisons can not go? Then one of the contact poisons or lice remedies is the proper thing to use. Is it a fungous trouble not caused by any insect? Then half-strength Bordeaux is probably best; or perhaps sulphur for mildew. Or if both insects and fungi are at work, try a combination of arsenate of lead and half-strength Bordeaux.

Some of the shrubs—notably the lilac—are very subject to a scale pest called the oyster-shell bark-louse. The scales can be plainly seen, without the aid of a glass, on the branches—brown in color and shaped something like an elongated oyster-shell. Remedy: Spray with the whale-oil soap solution about the middle of May. There is also a scurfy scale which looks like a tiny, oblong flake of cotton. Use same remedy as for oyster-shell scale. Last, but most dangerous, is the San Jose scale. This is a round, dark scale with a central dot or nipple, and is not easy to see without the aid of a magnifying glass. It attacks and kills many shrubs, osage orange hedges, trees, etc. The lime-sulphur mixture is the standard remedy for San Jose. Seedsmen sell it by the quart or gallon, ready-mixed. Or if you have many shrubs or trees affected, write to your state experiment station or to the U. S. Department of Agriculture, Washington, D. C., and ask for bulletins about making and spraying the lime-sulphur mixture. The time to use it is *after the leaves are off*—in the late fall or very early spring.

If the flower garden has a garden hose and water under pressure, most insects can be controlled by throwing the water forcibly all over the plants every day or so (but do not do this when the hot sun is shining on them). This knocks off nearly all kinds of bugs, lice, etc. (not scale insects), and they soon get discouraged and disappear.

CHAPTER XVII

SMALL FRUITS

The berry garden is just the place
Where summer lends peculiar grace.
What possibilities may lie
In things drawn from its rich supply!

FIRST, let us talk about strawberries. April is the best month in the North to set the plants. Select almost any kind of good, well-drained land on which some hoed crop was grown last season. The soil should be deeply plowed, enriched with manure and fertilizers and harrowed until fine and mellow. Dig or buy plants from beds set last season which have not yet fruited, so as not to get "little potato" runners from old, worn-out plants. Select well-tested varieties that do well in your climate and soil, and which are liked in your local markets. For horse cultivation many growers set the plants in rows about four feet apart, and about eighteen inches apart in the row (7,260 plants to the acre). Spread the roots out well and deep; tread the soil firmly about each plant; see that the crown of plant is level with ground, and uncovered but not too high; pick off all blossoms, runners, old and dead leaves, and keep blossoms and fruit off during the first season. When setting plants, avoid drying the roots by exposure to sun or wind, and reject all small, feeble, or old plants with dark-looking roots. Read Chapter III for general planting hints. Before setting, many growers practise shearing or cutting about one-third off the ends of all roots. Remember that strawberry plants are either pistillate (imperfect blossoms) or staminate (perfect). Most growers insure good fertilization of blossoms (without which the pistillate varieties can not produce fruit) by setting one row of a perfect-blossom variety, two rows of imperfect, then another row of perfect—and so on. As soon as the field is all planted, start the cultivator and loosen up the trodden soil. Hoe and cultivate the plants often but shallow. Arrange the runners by hand, spacing them properly and securing each one in place with a little soil or a small stone. When enough runners have rooted, cut off the surplus ones the same as if they were weeds. Aim to have the final row not more than eighteen inches wide, with plants spaced (irregularly) six to eight inches apart. Continue to hoe and cultivate until hard frosts come in the fall; then, when the soil is *well* frozen, mulch the rows or the entire field with clean straw, marsh hay, etc. In late March or early April, if the mulch on the strawberry bed is heavy and packed down, loosen it up a little and rake part of it into the aisles between the rows. I do not believe that it is best, usually, to cultivate or hoe the bed in the spring; simply pull up weeds that push through the mulch. If you want to keep the bed another year, says a writer in Farm Journal, after fruiting time mow off the plant leaves and tops, let them dry a day or so, and then set fire to dry leaves and mulch and burn it off. Choose a dry, windy day for this job, so that the fire will run *quickly* along the rows. As soon as the new growth starts, narrow down the rows by plowing one furrow away from each side, and then cultivate the soil back into place. Then treat the bed the same as the first year. When it has borne two crops, better plow it under.

The foregoing well-known method is what is called the "narrow matted row" system. Of course in a small garden, for hoe cultivation only, the rows might be closer together—say three feet and a half apart.

Sometimes the "wide matted row" method is used—allowing the plant row to become two or three feet wide. Then, last but not least, there's the "hill system" of culture—setting the plants about fifteen inches apart in rows about three feet apart, for horse cultivation, or in two-foot rows for hoe work only. Blossoms are kept off and all runners are promptly and regularly cut off all through the growing season, and the plants, not being exhausted by runner, blossom or fruit bearing, put all their strength into themselves and grow big, sturdy and bushy. Apply a mulch when the ground freezes, and look for a fine crop of extra-fancy berries the following June. This method requires high culture and fertilization to produce satisfactory results. Occasional applications of nitrate of soda the first season, and again the following spring after growth starts, are helpful. (Nitrate of soda is useful in any system of strawberry growing. See Chapter IV.)

Some folks advocate setting strawberries in August or early September. I prefer spring-set beds, but if you must set in the fall, use pot-grown plants and begin to prepare the ground a few weeks ahead of planting time. Plow it early so that it will have a chance to settle. Harrow or rake it often, to keep down weeds and conserve moisture. Then the bed

ONE WAY TO PROTECT BERRIES FROM BIRDS. THE WIRE-NETTING WILL LAST A LONG TIME, BUT OF COURSE THE PLAN IS NOT PRACTICABLE EXCEPT ON A SMALL SCALE

will be in fine shape to receive the plants. Pot-grown plants can be had of most nurserymen; or you can easily raise them yourself by buying a number of tiny pots, filling them with earth, sinking them alongside a new strawberry bed, and causing a runner to take root in each pot.

Strawberry varieties: There are hundreds of them. Every locality has its favorites. New kinds are constantly being introduced, and most old kinds sooner or later drop out of sight. I have only space to mention a few well-tested varieties which are general favorites in many places at the time of this writing ("P" means pistillate or imperfect blossoms, "S" means staminate or perfect blossoms): Bubach (P), Haverland (P), Clyde (S), Marshall (S), Warfield (P), Wm. Belt (S), Lovett (S), Nick Ohmer (S), Glen Mary (S), New York (S), Senator Dunlap (S), Klondike (S), Rough Rider (S), etc., etc. If you want extra early berries, regardless of size, plant Michel's Early (S), Tennessee Prolific (S), etc. For very late kinds, plant Gandy (S), Parker Earle (S), Brandywine (S), etc.

Picking and marketing: Do not pick strawberries when they are wet; when picked, hurry them to a cool place out of the sun; do not bruise; pick every ripe berry every day or two; do not jerk the berries off—nip them off at the stem; throw out over-ripe or under-ripe specimens. J. H. Hale says: "For distant

DO NOT PICK BERRIES FOR SHIPMENT WHEN THEY ARE WET, AND BE CAREFUL NOT TO BRUISE

market, try to pick in the evening or in the morning after the dew is off the grass and yet before it is too warm. If picking must be done all through the heat of the day, plan some way to cool the berries. Pickers of mature years are best; and as a rule girls are better than boys. Have a superintendent for every ten or twelve pickers, to assign the rows, inspect the picking, etc. Each picker should be numbered and have a picking stand or carrier with like number to hold four, six or eight quarts. Sort the berries as picked into two grades, and always use new, clean baskets made of the whitest wood possible. Fill rounding full with fruit of uniform quality all the way through. After berries are picked keep away from the air as much as possible. Fruit, if dry cooled, will keep much longer and keep fresher if kept in tight crates. Ventilation in crates and baskets does more harm than good." In many parts of the East the 32-quart crate is the favorite shipping package; in Michigan and some other states, the 16-quart gift-crate is popular (this kind is shown in the packing-shed illustration in this chapter).

Strawberry pests: Leaf-spot, blight, rust and mildew can all be largely controlled by early sprayings with the Bordeaux mixture. Rotation of crops and the annual "burning over" of each bed after it has fruited, will usually control the crown-borer, the leaf-roller, and similar insects; also, put some arsenate of lead in the Bordeaux mixture and use the combined spray until little green berries begin to form, then stop, and resume spraying after the fruiting season is over. White grubs (larvæ of May beetles or "June bugs" as they are sometimes called) often attack the roots below ground and the plant withers and dies; there are no good remedies, but fall-plowing and regular cultivation are preventives; never plant strawberries on ground which has been in sod within two or three years and you'll have little trouble with white grubs.

RASPBERRIES AND BLACKBERRIES.—To get a start, buy plants of a nurseryman; or propagate from an old patch, as follows: New plants of the red raspberry and blackberry may be obtained by digging the larger vigorous roots and cutting in pieces two or three i n c h e s in length, according to their size; the s m a l l e r the root the longer it should be cut. Cut the roots in the fall and store in boxes of sand placed in a dry, c o o l c e l l a r until spring. As soon as the ground can be properly prepared, scatter the root pieces thinly in furrows and c o v e r with two inches of light, loamy soil. Choose a moist, partially s h a d e d situation, keep clean and free from weeds, and by fall you

GET BERRIES OUT OF THE SUN AND INTO THE PACKING-SHED QUICKLY

will have a good supply of strong, healthy plants for early spring setting (for the North I favor spring setting). An easier way, is to dig suckers or sprouts that come up along or between the rows, being sure to secure with each sprout a short portion of the cross root from which it grew; dig and set these in permanent rows in the early spring. (Much of this digging, however, hurts a patch.)

Blackcap raspberries do not sucker from the roots and are propagated differently. When blackcap tips bend down near the ground toward autumn, new plants can be easily started. Bend down and bury each tip a few inches beneath the ground, holding it in place by pegs, a stone, or the weight of a little heaped-up soil. Most of the tips, if not disturbed, will take root and form nice plants by next spring; at which time the parent canes can be severed a few inches from the new plants, and the latter can then be dug up and set out wherever desired.

Planting-distances, culture, etc.: Blackberries for horse cultivation are usually set about eight feet apart in rows, plants spaced about two feet (2,722 to the acre). Red raspberry rows, about six feet apart, plants spaced about two feet (3,630 to the acre). The plants, of both, sucker and run together in the row in a year of two, until there is a continuous hedgerow about a foot wide (plants which come up outside of this should be treated like weeds). For small garden or hoe cultivation the rows might be a little closer together. Blackcaps for horse cultivation may be set in six-foot rows, about two and one-half feet apart between plants; or 5 x 5, and cultivated both ways if the rows are straight in each direction (1,742 plants to the acre). As blackcaps do not sucker, the hills will "stay put."

As to the depth to set plants of raspberries and blackberries, I shall simply say: Set them only a trifle deeper than they were before digging.

Soil for these berries should be moist, well fertilized, loamy, well drained and deeply plowed. Cultivation should begin in early spring and continue (say at ten-day intervals) until about the middle of August. A mulch at fruiting time is helpful and practicable in a small patch. A cover crop is sometimes sown at the last cultivation, for turning under in early spring. Do not plow the ground (after it is planted) deeper than three inches; cultivate about two inches deep; hand-hoe between plants where the cultivator can not go. Do not let plants produce fruit the first season; a small crop may be expected the following year; a full crop the third year.

Pruning: The first year, none. After that, cut out (close to the ground) all old canes each summer *as soon as they have fruited*. At the same time, cut out surplus canes (when the rows get too thick) and diseased or feeble canes. Remove and burn the cuttings, promptly. Don't let the rows get too wide or too thick, but be sure to leave *enough* new shoots for next year's fruiting. In the early spring go through the patch again; cut out all broken or winter-killed canes or branches, shorten remaining canes to four or five feet, and cut off at least a third of the tips of long side-shoots. Rake up and burn all brush. (NOTE: There is another pruning detail which is practised by some growers, called "summer pruning" or "pinching." This consists of pinching off the tip ends of all new shoots when they are not more than two feet high—the idea being to make the canes stocky and more self-supporting, with low side-branches. This method has advantages and disadvantages; some growers greatly favor it, while others condemn it and say that it often causes too much late, tender growth that winter-kills in the North. It seems to work better with blackcaps and blackberries, than with red raspberries.) If the canes are properly pruned, no supports should be needed; although in small gardens it is quite common to string stout wires along the rows, either using double wires or tying the canes to a single wire. Blackcaps and blackberries are usually picked and packed in quart boxes in crates the same as strawberries. Red raspberries are generally packed in *pint* boxes. Get blackberries out of the sun double-quick, or they'll turn red in spots, says Tim; and he speaks from experience.

Varieties: The following kinds of blackberries are hardy, or nearly so, in New York State, says O. M. Taylor: Agawam, Ancient Briton, Eldorado, Snyder, Ohmer, Stone Hardy, Taylor, Wachusett. The not hardy kinds are: Kittatinny, Lovett, Mersereau, Minnewaski, Wilson Jr., Early Harvest, Early Mammoth. (The latter varieties may endure the winter cold some years, but the safest way is to bend down the canes lengthwise of the row in late fall and cover with earth, in the extreme North; this bending is done by first removing some soil from one side of the roots.)

Gregg, Kansas, Ohio, Conrath, etc., are popular blackcaps. Cuthbert, Miller, Loudon, etc., are good red raspberries. (Golden Queen is a yellow-fruited variety. Shaffer is a purple-cap kind, but not popular for market.)

Insects and diseases: Cane-borers, gall-beetles, tree-crickets and similar insects that infest raspberry and blackberry canes, are difficult to combat with sprays; however, the prompt cutting out and burning of old, dead and infested canes will usually keep these enemies in check. A little worm (the larvæ of a black saw-fly) sometimes feeds upon the leaves; hellebore or arsenate of lead sprays will kill it. Anthracnose (purplish or scabby patches on the canes) is a fungous trouble; spray with the Bordeaux mixture and promptly destroy canes after fruiting. Red rust (powdery, orange-red places on leaves, etc.) is a very common trouble; dig out infested plants—root and branch—whenever seen, and burn; be careful not to scatter the dust on healthy bushes; early sprayings with Bordeaux may help a little.

CURRANTS AND GOOSEBERRIES.—Buy plants. Or, soon after the leaves fall in autumn, currant, gooseberry and grape cuttings may best be made. Use this season's new wood-growth; cut into lengths about eight inches long, tie into bundles, and bury in not too wet sand in the cellar, for spring planting. Or if you will mulch them well through the winter, they may be set at once in the fall. Set them slightly leaning, top end up, about five inches apart, deeply, in rows (each cutting having at least one bud above and one below ground), cultivate them as you would any other crop, and transplant them to their permanent place the following fall or spring. The soil should be well firmed around the cuttings.

Most growers make the permanent rows 5 x 5 feet and cultivate both ways; but in a small garden the bushes might be spaced about four feet apart in five-foot rows. A well-drained clay or clay-loam soil is liked best by these bushes. They are great feeders and manure should be used bountifully. The roots run close to the surface, so beware of cultivating deeply; but regular, light stirrings of the soil until August are beneficial. Some growers cultivate the ground once or twice in the spring and then mulch the surface during the balance of the year; this is a good hint for the small gardener. In some localities currants and gooseberries are packed in quart boxes the same as strawberries; consult your local market-

man.   Gooseberries are usually marketed while in a
green, hard condition.

Pruning and pests: These fruits are usually
grown and trained in bush form, and shoots from
the base are utilized to renew the top gradually.
Pruning consists of cutting out weak or superfluous
new shoots, and old ones which have outlived their
usefulness or which have become diseased or infested
with borers.   But never cut out too many old stalks
at once, for the bulk of the fruit is produced on such
wood.   Stalks may be left until about three years
old—which is often the limit of their usefulness.
All shoots, old or new, may be cut back, as desired,
to make the bushes more compact and symmetrical,
and the fruit larger.   In other words, thin out, cut
back, and gradually replace the older stalks with
younger ones.   Burn all clippings promptly, for thus
the borer is kept down.   The principal other enemy
is the currant worm which attacks the leaves in early
spring.   Remedy: Spray the bushes with the hellebore mixture given in Chapter V, but do it promptly
when the first worm is seen; watch the bushes
closely shortly after the leaves unfold in the spring.
Fungous blight troubles can be controlled with Bordeaux.   Sulphur for mildew is often used.

Varieties: Victoria, Cherry, Fay's Prolific, etc.,
are popular kinds of currants.   Red Dutch is the
small, old-fashioned kind; it is still much grown.
White Dutch and White Grape are white varieties.
Black Naples is esteemed for jellies, etc.   Downing,
Houghton, Columbus, etc., are well-known native
gooseberries.   Industry is a fine, large European
variety, very sweet; but more subject to mildew
than the American kinds.

GRAPES.—Buy one-year-old vines; or propagate

them from cuttings as advised for currants (page 177). Vineyard rows should be about eight feet apart, plants spaced about eight feet in the rows. Any good, well-drained soil will do, but—commercially speaking—grapes do their best only in certain localities where temperature, climate, etc., are entirely favorable. The "Chautauqua grape belt" in New York state is such a place. There are others. However, a few grapes for home use can be grown almost anywhere. On account of greater security against frost dangers, an elevated location is preferable to a low-lying place. In very cold sections grapes do especially well on the sunny side of a wall, fence or building. So be sure to have at least a few Concords, Delawares, Niagaras, Brightons, etc. After planting, cut back the top to about three buds and let the vine grow as it pleases the first season. Then, the next February, cut back the best cane to about four "eyes" or buds, and cut off any other canes entirely; when these buds commence to grow, rub off all but the two strongest shoots, and, as they grow, tie them to the wire of a trellis or to a stake. The third year's pruning will depend somewhat upon what system of training you decide upon; the subject is too large and intricate for treatment here. The Kniffen system is one often used; it consists in training the vine so that it has four horizontal side or main branches, two on each side, one above another, tied to two wires; the first wire may be about three feet high, the second about five feet. I suggest that every grape-grower should send to the U. S. Department of Agriculture, Washington, D. C., ask for free Farmers' Bulletins Nos. 156 and 284, and learn all the facts about other systems.

Extra-fine grapes are obtained by cutting off the

inferior bunches and removing those that crowd others. Cultivation, too, helps to make fine fruit. So do annual applications of bone meal, stable manure, and some form of potash. Another aid to high quality, is "sacking" or "bagging" the bunches. The best time to do this is when the berries are quite small—not larger than small shot. Ordinary two-pound paper sacks can be used. The mouth of each sack should be snugly wrapped around the stem of the bunch, and securely held in place by pinning or tying. The tie should be tight, but, of course, not too tight. The sacks protect the grapes from fungous and insect enemies, including wasps, birds, etc., and the bunches thus protected are finer and more perfect. For grape-rot and mildew, begin early and spray the vines with Bordeaux mixture at intervals of about two weeks. The addition of arsenate of lead to the earlier sprayings will kill any insects which eat the leaves (see Chapter V).

OTHER FRUITS.—In regard to the dewberry, etc., I must refer you to my Berry Book. There, also, you will find many details about small-fruit growing which lack of space excludes from this chapter.

INDEX